CHICAGO SHAKESPEARE THEATER

CHICAGO
Shakespeare
THEATER

Suiting the Action to the Word

Edited by Regina Buccola and Peter Kanelos

NIU PRESS / *DeKalb, IL*

© 2013, 2015 by Northern Illinois University Press
Published by the Northern Illinois University Press, DeKalb, Illinois 60115
Manufactured in the United States using acid-free paper
First printing in paperback, 2015
All rights reserved
Design by Shaun Allshouse

Unless otherwise noted, all photos, images, and architectural drawings are courtesy of Chicago
Shakespeare Theater.

Library of Congress Cataloging-in-Publication Data
Chicago Shakespeare Theater : suiting the action to the word / edited by Regina Buccola and
Peter Kanelos.
    pages   cm
  ISBN 978 0 87580 467 5 (hardback)
  ISBN 978 0 87580 685 3 (paperback)
  ISBN 978 1 60909 070 8 (e book)
  1. Chicago Shakespeare Theater. 2. Shakespeare, William, 1564–1616—Stage history—Illinois—
Chicago 3. Theatrical companies—Illinois—Chicago. 4. Theater—Illinois—Chicago—History.
I. Buccola, Regina, 1969– II. Kanelos, Peter, 1971–
  PR3105.C48 2012
  822.3'3—dc23
  2012045333

Contents

CONTENTS

Acknowledgments

As we write this, scarcely a year has passed since the idea for this collection took shape. One does not make so rapid a journey from inception to execution without incurring more debts of gratitude than can readily be repaid in a few paragraphs of prose. To fail in the attempt, however, seems better than to fail to attempt it.

First and foremost, we must express our gratitude to Chicago Shakespeare Theater itself, which demonstrated once again its unique position in the cultural landscape by virtue of the unique relationship in which it has stood to us and to our contributors, offering free access to archives, artists, and administrators while at the same time agreeing to have absolutely no editorial control over the resulting essays. While everyone at the theater has been tremendously helpful, particular thanks are due to Barbara Gaines, Criss Henderson, Marilyn Halperin, Alida Szabo, Chris Plevin, Elizabeth Neukirch, Julie Stanton, and Jonathan Baude, who gave very generously of their time and energy during a theater season that taxed those resources to an exceeding degree. Any factual errors or other infelicities that remain in the volume are entirely our responsibility, and none of theirs.

Second, all of the contributors to this volume are to be thanked for their strong commitment to the project. The alacrity and goodwill with which everyone assayed the tasks at hand has been remarkable. The tight time line for this project meant that not everyone who was willing to contribute was able; for support, advice, and recommendations of contributors, we are grateful to Will West, Jeff Masten, Garry Wills, Lisa Freeman, Mary Beth

Rose, Suzanne Gossett, Richard Strier, and Stuart Sherman. Beth Charlebois deserves special mention for her thoughtful and protracted e-mail correspondence with Regina Buccola about the PreAmble lecture series.

Finally, thanks are due to our family and friends, who sacrificed a great deal of quality time with us at two major holidays while we wrapped up this project.

To all, thanks, and evermore thanks.

R.B. and P.K.

CHICAGO SHAKESPEARE THEATER

Introduction
Regina Buccola and Peter Kanelos

"THE ACCOMPLISHMENT OF MANY YEARS"

Overcoming the clank of "L" trains, the thunder of overflying jets and even the occasional odors from a nearby back-yard fish fry, 17 performers enact 45 parts and serve up the heroic sweep of a major chapter in English history. Their tiny platform space plays home to battlefield carnage and coy royal courtship, to knavish fooleries and kingly crises, to senseless bloodshed and to lusty victory, all in a production that's as economic as it is well-spoken and affecting.[1]

Sid Smith could scarcely have realized when he wrote his review of the Chicago Shakespeare Workshop's production of *Henry V* in 1986 that he was witnessing the prologue to a major chapter in Chicago theater history. The muse of fire that inhabited that production's director, Barbara Gaines, had provided only a pub rooftop for a stage, enthusiastic Shakespeare greenhorns to act, and adventurous audiences who spent more on beer than they did on tickets (the production was performed gratis) to behold the swelling scene. By 1999 that unworthy scaffold had become a fond memory to the world-class Chicago Shakespeare Theater. To tell that story, we must jump "o'er times, / Turning the accomplishment of many years / Into an hour-glass: for the which supply, / Admit me Chorus to this history."[2]

1. Poster for William Shakespeare's *Henry V* (1986), directed by Barbara Gaines—the production mounted on the rooftop of the Red Lion Inn that launched Shakespeare Repertory Company, renamed Chicago Shakespeare Theater on Navy Pier in 1999.

Chicago Shakespeare Theater is the brainchild of Gaines, who has served as Artistic Director throughout the theater's twenty-five-year history. A graduate of Northwestern University's theater program, Gaines garnered early acclaim as an actress in Chicago before heading to New York City.[3] Gaines returned to Chicago in 1980 and started teaching Shakespearean performance in the basement of what was then the Organic Theater while she recovered from knee surgery in 1983. Gaines started (as she does today) with table work using the texts in the First Folio (1623), the first collected edition of Shakespeare's plays, published by his theatrical partners, John Heminges and Henry Condell. A year later, Gaines and her band of Shakespeare students/actors staged a Shakespeare Showcase at Victory Gardens Theater; by the time of a second showcase at The Second City in 1985, the group had grown substantially, and Gaines had a mission statement:

> Our goal is to establish a world-class Shakespeare Repertory Company and training center in Chicago, which will provide work for our artists and culturally nourish the people of our city.
>
> This theater would become an international center for the arts, attracting talent from all over the world, while always keeping its commitment to and dependence upon the artists, directors and craftsman [*sic*] of Chicago.[4]

What sounded like an audacious set of goals at the time now reads like a checklist of the work that Chicago Shakespeare Theater routinely does today.

To take the fledgling company from showcases to full-length productions, Gaines relied on her extensive network within the Chicago theater community. "I asked Victory Gardens for rehearsal space; they said yes. I asked the Goodman Theater if we could build in their shop; they said yes," said Gaines, ticking off the early supporters on her fingers.[5] John Cordwell, owner of the Red Lion Pub in Chicago's Lincoln Park, agreed to let the Shakespeare Workshop stage *Henry V* on the pub's roof. The lone snag came from the Actors' Equity Association, which refused to let the actors who held equity cards perform without pay. The plan for the production had been to ask the audience only for donations. "I thought 'Gee, that's odd— we're trying to start a theater,'" Gaines recalled. "So, a bunch of actors—I was one—went to a meeting and pointed out that a dark theater is a dark theater. So they reversed their decision; they did the right thing, eventually."[6]

The play ran for two weeks to popular and critical acclaim; standing-room only crowds thronged around the jammed bleacher seating. Gaines swears that the meteorological implications of performing on the roof of a pub did not occur to her until she woke up on the morning of opening night—August 3rd 1986, my mother's birthday—with a chill wondering if it would rain for the next two weeks, because then we wouldn't have a Shakespeare theater in Chicago. Of course it did rain on the buildings next door, but it never did rain on the roof at the Red Lion Pub. Nothing was canceled, all of our patrons saw it, and many of them joined the board.[7]

Although they had passed the hat at *Henry V* like a band of itinerant players, the Shakespeare Workshop did not have to rely for long on what they could pull out of it. As luck would have it, Gaines had, through a friend, a connection with a man who worked at Chase Manhattan Bank. One day, Gaines remembered, "I get a phone call from the New York office: 'We hear you're trying to start a Shakespeare theater; we're going to send you $10,000 in seed money.' So finally we had a bank account. Over the course of the next year, we collected over $90,000—which is a hell of a lot of money."[8] That money went into an account bearing the new name of the company: Shakespeare Repertory Company, or as it would come to be known in shorthand, Shakespeare Rep.

The newly christened company also acquired a new place in which to perform: the Ruth Page Dance Center in Chicago's Gold Coast. Shakespeare Rep's first play in its new home was *Troilus and Cressida*, which premiered in October 1987. Like *Henry V* the year before, the production received many positive reviews. Slowly building momentum, the theater stuck to one production per year initially, staging *Antony and Cleopatra* in 1988, and *Cymbeline* in 1989. In a stroke of fate well suited to the preposterous divine interventions of the play itself, one of the people shut out of the packed house to see *Cymbeline* was Criss Henderson, who had just completed his studies in the Theatre School at DePaul University. Identifying him as the company's "entrepreneurial founding father—a visionary entrepreneur," Gaines lost no time securing him as managing director of Shakespeare Rep.[9] The partnership lasts to this day; Henderson remains at the helm of Chicago Shakespeare Theater as Executive Director.

Within the next five years, the company grew exponentially. First came a pair of two-play seasons: *King John* and *Much Ado About Nothing* in 1991, followed by *Pericles* and *Macbeth* in 1992. In the spring of 1992, Shakespeare Repertory launched "Team Shakespeare," its educational outreach program, which brought a new administrator on board: Marilyn Halperin, Director of Education and Communications. "The best thing I ever did was hire Marilyn," Criss Henderson declared. "We say that Marilyn was the first professional we ever hired; up to that point we just had a couple of kids in an apartment office—I was a kid myself," Henderson laughed.[10]

2. Greg Vinkler and Frank Nall in *King John* (1991), directed by Barbara Gaines. Photo by Jennifer Girard

At Henderson's suggestion, the company downsized back to a single production, *King Lear*, in 1993 in order to brace for the its next leap—to a three-play subscription series in 1993–1994. "We backed up in order to get a running start," Gaines explained. A crucial component of that running start was the performance of Richard Kneeland as King Lear. "I did summer stock with him and Rue McLanahan," Gaines recalled. "When we came to do *Lear*, I'd been following Richard's career but hadn't seen him in years. Miraculously, Richard said yes, and saved the theater's life—his performance was so spectacular."[11] Fans of *Slings and Arrows* know that importing a celebrated elder statesman to play the role of Lear doesn't always end happily. For Shakespeare Repertory, however, the production poised the company for critical and commercial success in its first three-play season, with *Cymbeline*, *The Taming of the Shrew*, and *Measure for Measure*. By 1995, the company had added an abridged production of *Romeo and Juliet* to its three-play season (*The Winter's Tale*, *Troilus and Cressida*, and *As You Like It*); in addition to performances at the Ruth Page, the abridgment toured schools throughout the state.

Before its tenth-anniversary season, the basic elements that would carry through from Shakespeare Repertory to Chicago Shakespeare Theater were all in place: three-play seasons on the main stage; robust educational programming, complemented by plays that catered to student audiences and to the unique demands of statewide touring; and visiting actors and directors of international renown, like Kneeland, and David Gilmore, who directed *As You Like It* in 1994. By its tenth-anniversary season in 1996, Shakespeare Repertory had become Chicago's third-largest nonprofit theater company.

"The nineties was a renaissance in Chicago with respect to arts and culture," Henderson reflected. "[Mayor] Daley's platform, [Richard] Christiansen and the power of the *Tribune*—probably more than any other city, in Chicago there was a disproportionately high number of people going to the theater. People attribute that cultural growth and success to the theaters, but it didn't come from us, actually. It came from the audience."[12]

"We grew so fast," Gaines mused. "We were probably the fastest-growing theater in America."[13] By the mid-1990s, Shakespeare Repertory was in fact expanding so rapidly that it was outgrowing its home at the Ruth Page Dance Center. The administrative offices outgrew the Ruth Page space first and moved to another location a few blocks away. Architectural plans and protracted negotiations with the City of Chicago and the Metropolitan Pier and Exposition Authority began in 1997, ultimately producing a set of agreements that allowed the theater to move to its current location on Navy Pier in 1999, taking on the new name of Chicago Shakespeare Theater. Like every other aspect of the theater's growth, the construction of the six-story theater on Navy Pier moved at lightning speed. The groundbreaking ceremony took place on September 29, 1998. In less than a year, the theater was occupied, with actors rehearsing *Antony and Cleopatra* in their spacious new rehearsal rooms, and administrative staff admonished to wear hard hats into the fifth-floor restrooms as construction crews put finishing touches on the fly system.

Much like the shift from a one-play season to a three-play season, Chicago Shakespeare Theater's move from cramped quarters at the Ruth Page Dance Center to its own six-floor, 75,000-square-foot purpose-built space on Navy Pier was a quantum leap. However, as Henderson observed, the lessons learned at Ruth Page served Chicago Shakespeare well when it moved to its new home on the Pier:

> At Ruth Page we were presenting these works at a high level with such limited resources. We developed "producorial" muscle. Once we had the ability to produce Shakespeare at that level, then anything we put the artistic enterprise toward was coming out at that high quality, and was being supported. It didn't really matter who the playwright was, there was something Shakespearean in the way we were making work. We were not rough-and-tumble. There is an aspiration here fueled by the theatrical standard of excellence that Shakespeare sets that has contributed to the work every day for the past twenty-five years.[14]

While it may not initially seem intuitive to see *Peter Pan* or Steven Sondheim's *Pacific Overtures* on the roster at Chicago *Shakespeare* Theater, the theater's commitment to producing work that meets a "Shakespearean" standard in terms of production values and aesthetic sensibilities renders these choices coherent for the theater. "All of the work that we do—the children's programming, the musicals, the plays by other playwrights—all sits comfortably together," Henderson explained.[15]

"International, children, Shakespeare—that is it," Gaines summed up the theater's mission. "I'd close the theater before I'd cut the children's programming and the international work."[16] Children's programming is of vital importance to Gaines and Henderson insofar as those children constitute the theater audience of the future. When in July 2011 we discussed the theater's first twenty-five years, Chicago Shakespeare Theater had just begun previews of its summer production, *Pinocchio*. "You see these kids—four, five, six years old—and they are seeing their first theatrical production and falling in love with theater," Gaines exclaimed.

In addition to family-friendly productions like *Pinocchio* (2011) or *Joseph and the Amazing Technicolor Dreamcoat* (2000), overseen by Rick Boynton, Creative Producer, in the summer months when many other Chicago theaters are dark, the theater also presents abbreviated versions of Shakespeare's plays intended for family audiences during the regular theater season. Plays in the "Short Shakespeare" series are designed to be family-friendly, with run times of approximately seventy-five minutes.[17] A handful of Shakespeare's plays logically lend themselves to the "Short Shakespeare" format and recur much more frequently than shows typically return to the main stage. *Macbeth, The Comedy of Errors,* and *The Taming of the Shrew* share the virtue of being relatively short plays, requiring fewer editorial interventions to streamline than other plays in the Shakespeare canon. The tragedies *Macbeth* and *Romeo and Juliet* are frequently assigned texts in middle schools and high schools and therefore also appear routinely, creating a clear connection between preexisting lesson plans and the opportunity to bring a class to the theater for a field trip. However, each reiteration of a Short Shakespeare play involves a new production.

Education programming at the theater divides into three main areas, under the purview of Marilyn Halperin: the aforementioned "Short Shakespeare" productions each season catered to elementary, middle, and high school students; the wide range of support provided to teachers who bring their students to see productions of the plays; and "PreAmble" lectures offered before matinee performances of the main stage shows to general audiences by Chicago-area scholars. Area teachers are supported in three main ways by the theater's ambitious "Team Shakespeare" program launched in 1993: through the wealth of resources in the on-site Teacher Resource Center, through teaching guides and online resources prepared and published by the Education Program's staff, and through "Teacher Workshops" held on Saturdays just prior to the opening of each main stage and "Short Shakespeare" production. The workshops orient teachers to scholarly views of the play and how the production engages with that conversation, offer classroom exercises that can be used to engage students with the play and its language, and provide unique access to the rehearsal process for the production and the director's vision of the play. Chicago Shakespeare Theater offers teachers rare behind-the-scenes opportunities to survey the set and costume design plans, watch the actors in rehearsal, and meet the director for a discussion of the production.

Beth Charlebois, Associate Professor of English at St. Mary's College of Maryland, crafted the genre of the PreAmble lecture at Chicago Shakespeare Theater with the advice of Marilyn Halperin; Charlebois still trains the team of scholars who deliver these preshow talks to greater numbers of theatergoers each season. The thirty-minute lectures are designed to introduce theatergoers to significant aspects of the play and to highlight particular elements of the theater's production, all without "spoiling" surprising plot twists or arresting moments in the staging. "I think the best thing about the PreAmbles is that they give the audience not only a background on the play but a way of understanding the significance of the artistic choices that they are about to witness in performance—as choices that have implications," Charlebois contended.[18] While relevant historical context and issues of scholarly concern (such as the exploration of socially prescribed gender roles in *Twelfth Night* or *As You Like It*) do come in for consideration in the PreAmble format, the main emphasis of the lectures falls on production choices: sound design, costuming, lighting effects, period setting, and significant stage business.

Underscoring the extent to which PreAmbles are not meant to be purely didactic, Henderson stressed, "We didn't want people to have to prepare to come to the show; we're putting on shows for everyday people." He linked the inclusiveness of Chicago Shakespeare Theater's productions to its presence in the heart of Chicago's downtown tourism hub, noting "the good sense that we made of the theater at the center of Navy Pier: the people's theater on the people's pier inspired by the people's playwright. The audience is always part of the process from start to finish. Our goal is not to be revisionist, to show how smart we are in these texts; we're show people—like Shakespeare. I think we're structured differently than people realize. We're just show people putting on a play, like he was."[19]

Chicago Shakespeare Theater has played well on its home turf over the years, frequently nominated in numerous categories for the Joseph Jefferson Awards, one of the highest honors in the Chicago theater community. Moreover, an impressive number of those nominations have yielded awards. In 2011 alone Chicago Shakespeare Theater carted home seven awards, including the top honors for a production, *The Madness of George III*, which also earned the awards for director (Penny Metropulos) and principal actor (Harry Groenor). In the past decade, however, the theater has begun to earn accolades worldwide. Associate Artistic Director Gary Griffin's *Pacific Overtures* toured to London, where it received the 2004 Olivier Award for outstanding musical production. In 2008, Chicago Shakespeare Theater received the Regional Theatre Tony Award, a form of recognition that, paradoxically, renders a regional theater significant well beyond its region.

Chicago Shakespeare Theater has found all the world its stage even as it invites all the world to its stage. Henderson identified its World's Stage Series as "one of the great joys of my work here." For her part, Gaines noted, "I actually wrote into the first mission that we do international work, both touring our own work, and attracting it to us."[20] In 2006, Chicago Shakespeare Theater met the former objective when it took a remount of Gaines's celebrated 1999 production of the two parts of *Henry IV*, which had closed out the company's tenure at the Ruth Page Dance Center, to the Royal Shakespeare Company for its "Complete Works" season.

Meanwhile, Chicago Shakespeare Theater has met the second aspect of its international mission by consistently attracting work of the first order from around the world. "Because Shakespeare is the world's playwright it makes sense to look at the plays of the world, since they have all been shaped

3. Nathan Hosner, Mark D. Hines, and Harry Groener in *The Madness of George III* (2011), by Alan Bennett, directed by Penny Metropolus. Photo by Liz Lauren

or informed in some way by Shakespeare," Henderson reasoned.[21] In the past five years alone, Chicago audiences have been treated to a vibrant array of international productions: Tim Supple's *A Midsummer Night's Dream* (2008), featuring actors, dancers, martial arts experts, and street acrobats from India and Sri Lanka performing the play's text in equal parts English and the seven South Asian dialects native to the cast; *Farewell Umbrella* (*Au revoir parapluie*, 2007), during which an audience seated primarily on floor pillows breathlessly watched an acrobatic production designed by James Thiérrée, Charlie Chaplin's grandson; *Water Fools* (*Fous de bassin*, 2009), which transported the audience to bleachers set up on the easternmost edge of Navy Pier to watch members of Ilotopie (France) ride bicycles on the surface of the lake, occasionally accompanied by an overstuffed taxicab, horn blaring, and a towering bewigged and bejeweled opera singer reminiscent of Marie Antoinette, among other aquatic anomalies; and the National Theatre of Scotland's *Black Watch* (2011) staged at a former armory on the north side of Chicago, where new recruits played pool on a table that metamorphosed into a terrifying cross between the Trojan Horse and a clown car, as a knife sliced through its seemingly solid surface and an impossible number of lethal fighters spilled silently out.

Running through a list of some of his own favorite productions in the World's Stage Series, Henderson marveled, "To have the Comédie Française [Molière's *Le malade imaginaire*], to have the Abbey [*The Playboy of the Western World*] on our stage, Peter Brook's *Hamlet*—I can't help but think that the brick walls of this theater were seasoned by Brook's production."[22] Reflecting on the ghosts of Brook's production moved Henderson to think about the ghosts that inhabited the inaugural production of the twenty-fifth-anniversary season, Gary Griffin's production of Steven Sondheim's *Follies*: "All of those ghosts—I like to think that the spirits of all of the productions live here in a more positive way [than the fractious and troublemaking ghosts of Sondheim's play]—perhaps less scantily clad and with fewer feathers."[23]

4. In foreground, Archana Ramaswamy and P R Jijoy in Dash Arts' *A Midsummer Night's Dream* (2008), director Tim Supple. Photo by Tristram Kenton

5. Kaori Ito in *Farewell Umbrella (Au Revoir, Parapluie)* (2008), directed by James Thiér-rée. Photo by Richard Haughton

"The most surprising thing to me is not looking back; it's looking forward—the idea that there is a permanence to what we built is never something that we were looking for. We didn't do any of the work that we did in search of permanence," Henderson concluded. "Now, I'm relatively confident that decades and decades and decades will go by and audiences will continue to have the opportunity to see the work that we do here. There is a DNA to the company; the worldview will change with the next leadership team, but the great storytelling will remain."[24]

IMAGINARY FORCES AT WORK

In its first twenty-five years, Chicago Shakespeare Theater not only has established itself as one of Chicago's premier cultural institutions but has garnered a reputation for excellence and innovation that extends across the world. Like Chicago, CST has gone global. In fact, Chicago Shakespeare Theater was the only American company to participate in the Globe to Globe 2012 festival at Shakespeare's Globe in London, a six-week-long event serving as a precursor to the 2012 London Cultural Olympiad, in which all of Shakespeare's thirty-seven plays will be presented, each by a separate international company and each in a different language. The selection of CST for this honor is an indicator not only of the theater's prestige but that its work is seen, from an international perspective, as representative of Shakespeare on the American stage and as distinguished in the English-speaking world. Twenty-five years after conjuring its first production on the "unworthy scaffold" of a rooftop of a pub in Chicago, Chicago Shakespeare Theater is again bringing its own swelling scene to Shakespeare's "wooden O."

Today, critics from across the globe carefully attend to what is happening on Navy Pier. Theater companies from around the world are eager to collaborate with CST. Celebrated directors and actors of international repute work frequently on its stage. What this volume seeks to do, however, is to look beyond accolades and the fruits of accomplishment, to trace the impact of the theater as a social, cultural, and artistic institution. Perched above the waters of Lake Michigan, the work of CST ripples outward. To follow its trajectories, we have gathered in this collection a variety of voices, from actors and critics to scholars and the public. Our hope is that by providing a broad perspective from which to evaluate and appreciate Chicago Shakespeare Theater, the pages of this collection might turn into an hourglass the accomplishment of many years.

In Part I of this volume, we look at some of the fundamental components that have shaped Chicago Shakespeare Theater. Terry Teachout, the drama

6. Ilotopie's *Water Fools (Fous de Bassin)* (2009). Photo by Klaus Tummers

critic for the *Wall Street Journal*, describes in "Chicago First" his initial encounter with CST, as well as subsequent experiences with the company. Tasked with covering the expansive landscape of American regional theater, Teachout, a New York–based critic, found his encounters with the work of CST transformative: "After my first few visits, I realized that what I was seeing was not just a theater company but a theatrical concept, a modern approach to the classics fully in accord with my own developing sense of what American regional theater at its best is all about."

Regina Buccola in her essay examines the formative influence upon this theatrical concept—Artistic Director, Barbara Gaines. In "Catapulting Shakespeare into the Present: The Artistic Vision of Barbara Gaines," Buccola follows Gaines's career from the founding of the first company in Chicago dedicated to performing the works of Shakespeare to leading the multifaceted theatrical institution that exists today. Gaines's directorial vision, which she describes as "humanist," is imprinted on the company in all its pursuits. In accord with this human-centered focus, Buccola explains, Gaines has always been attracted to Shakespeare's "problem plays"; the reasons she gives are very much in line with her deep sensitivity to the human condition: "I am interested in complexity, problems that can't be solved, the mystery inside of all of us." It is not surprising that as a result of such concerns a robust sense of community has emerged within the company, as well as the commitment to the larger community that is a hallmark of CST.

Jonathan Abarbanel, a critic and educator with an encyclopedic knowledge of theater in Chicago, has known Gaines since they were both teenagers and provides a playful look at Gaines's early years in the theater and beyond, in "Barbara, Shakespeare, and Me." Abarbanel has had a front-row seat to the evolution of CST from its founding days, and he has consistently remained an admirer. Gaines's approach to Shakespeare—pragmatic, down-to-earth—put the "Chicago" in Chicago Shakespeare Theater, Abarbanel notes, by shaking off stale conventions of performance while holding fast to the core integrity of the plays. He describes what was to him, accustomed as he had been to highly stylized "British" Shakespeare, the CST's revelatory approach to the language: "Make sense of the words *first* as expressions of character and intention, and the flow of the language will follow. And speak the speech, I pray you, as well-trained American actors (or Canadian actors, for that matter), not as well-trained American actors trying to sound British."

It is not only the principles and practices of theater artists that have shaped the plays performed by CST, according to Jonathan Walker, but the material theater itself. In "The Spatial Rhetoric of Chicago Shakespeare Theater,"

Walker applies the concept of "spatial rhetoric" to CST's main playing space, the Courtyard Theater, which he defines as the capacity to "construct dramatic meaning for their audiences not only through the delivery of dialogue, the blocking of actors, stage and costume design, and so on, but also through a calculated staging of space, which taps into a vocabulary of physical placement and juxtaposition to express both dramatic conflict and harmony, division and alliance, and detachment and intimacy among the characters who populate its stage." Analyzing several productions, Walker shows how the Courtyard's particular spatial configuration—a combined thrust and proscenium stage—has often been used by directors as an active component of productions.

A collection dedicated to Chicago Shakespeare Theater must acknowledge and examine the educational and outreach efforts that are central to its mission. Part II of this volume begins with Alicia Tomasian's account of Josie Rourke's 2009 *Twelfth Night*. Tomasian, a professor at a Chicago-area community college, found this production to be a provocative introduction to Shakespeare for her community-college students, and she reads Rourke's production through their responses to the play.

CST's commitment to its audience extends to nurturing new generations of playgoers through "Short Shakespeare!" a series that adapts Shakespeare's plays with younger viewers in mind. Since this endeavor is as idealistic as it is practical, CST eschews simplifying or popularizing the plays; rather, it insists that each production is a fully realized artistic work, ensuring that it is still Shakespeare that these audiences are getting. Like Tomasian, Jeffrey Gore finds at CST an appealing entrée into Shakespeare, in this case, for his own children. "Short Shakespeare! and the Corruption of the Young" relates Gore's experiences taking his daughters to see the 2008 *Romeo and Juliet*, directed by Amanda Dehnert. Impressed by the vivacity exhibited by the young audience during the Q&A session following, Gore reflected on the impact of CST's efforts to reach out past their subscription base: "This group of schoolchildren, who might normally be playing Nintendo or attending soccer practice on a Saturday morning, get to have an experience with their parents and schoolteachers, devoted actors, and everyone who is normally backstage holding together this messy 'conspiracy' of education, entertainment, and a thriving cultural enterprise. And a few of them just might get hooked and become fans and customers for life." Peter Sagal, National Public Radio personality, also reflects upon the efficacy of Short Shakespeare! in "Doing Things with Words . . . and, Sometimes, Swords." Sagal's experience teaching Shakespeare to seniors has made him realize that Shakespeare's work has at its heart a quality that appeals to young and old alike: "that is, as active, enacted depictions of human beings doing things. Shakespeare's genius, it seemed to me, was not so much his poetry as his sense of motivation, and how people acted upon one another." It is by distilling this essence that Short Shakespeare! manages to be both short and Shakespeare.

While Chicago Shakespeare Theater has been and remains very much an institution grounded in Chicago, a product of the city's rich theatrical tradition, CST frequently hosts guest artists from across the nation and the world. Part III explores the ways in which directors, actors, and playwrights have found this crucible to be a site of particular inspiration. Celebrated British thespian Simon Callow describes in "Chicago Shakespeare" the experience of stepping into the Courtyard: "When I did, I felt what every actor who has ever stood or worked in it must feel—an absolute rightness. The space holds you, it gives you focus and freedom. The energy lines converge with huge dynamic power, but at the same time, you're speaking to the audience as if they're in your front room." This sense of intimacy that fosters the establishment of direct relationships is one of the features often remarked upon by those who come to CST, either as actors or as audience. Such relationships are also cultivated backstage and behind the scenes. In "Chicago Shakespeare Theater and the Canadians," Richard Ouzounian, drama critic for the *Toronto Star*, chronicles the many dynamic alliances between theater artists from "up north" and CST. Such collaborations have proven to be a potent combination; as Ouzounian writes of Terry Hands's 2006 *Hamlet*: "Even though it had a Canadian lead and a British director, I think of it as the archetypal Chicago show: played with power, clarity and emotional honesty like you really don't see in any other city."

Collaboration is the issue at the crux of Gina Marie Di Salvo's essay, "The Framing of the Shrew." For its 2010 production, directed by Josie Rourke, CST commissioned the controversial, often inflammatory, playwright Neil LaBute, to refashion the Induction that frames the action of *Taming of the Shrew*. Di Salvo relates the very complex effect that this had on the production, both during the rehearsal process and once the play opened: "LaBute's script called for depicting the problematic story of Katherina's taming as conventionally as possible and used the frame to move the sexual politics out of the realm of traditional heterosexist hierarchies. Instead of representing the problem of widespread and ongoing societal misogyny, LaBute moved the conversation of *Shrew* into the realm of personal and particular abuses of power." In ways that echo Kate's resistance to Petruchio's efforts to "tame" her, the cast and audience pushed back against LaBute's interpolations, providing particularly apt responses to the provocative choices made by both the playwright and the theater.

Resistance to convention has always been a feature of the work of Michael Bogdanov, including his 2003 CST production of *The Winter's Tale*. While it has been customary for directors (and scholars) to try to find ways to fuse together the radically disparate halves of the play—the world of jealousy, recrimination, and death that is found in Sicilia with the realm of amity, trust, and fertility found in Bohemia—Bogdanov refused facile compromise, according to Bradley Greenburg: "Bogdanov's approach to the play is to contrast the two sites and times of the drama as dual genre-specific spaces: Sicilia & tragedy, Bohemia & comedy. If he rejects the 'romance' label, he does so by attending to the play's paradox as a productive source for what is a realistic set of conflicts." Greenburg argues, in "Michael Bogdanov: An International Director's *The Winter's Tale* at Chicago Shakespeare Theater," that by allowing the two parts of the play to remain in tension with each other, the possibility for a final reconciliation emerges, not within the action of the play but following it, through the marriage of Perdita and Florizel, and that this choice accords with Bogdnaov's political approach to all of his work, which is ultimately not didactic but dialectical.

Taking chances, bucking conventions—these are also themes explored by Clark Hulse in "Risky Business: *Rose Rage* at Chicago Shakespeare Theater." Edward Hall's 2003 *Rose Rage*, a conflation of *Henry VI, Parts 1, 2*, and *3*, was an immensely ambitious and risky production, a massive, intricate narrative enacted within the confines of a virtual slaughterhouse, running the good part of a day, and featuring a meal during the break. Hulse catalogues the obstacles that Hall and CST were compelled to face:

> Would audiences be willing to commit six hours to the production, plus travel time to and from the theater? Would anybody want to sit down to a meal in the midst of the butchery and mayhem? Could the actors maintain the stamina and focus to put the show on four times a week? Could the set withstand a constant pounding with knives and staves, and would the stage floor—slippery with blood and offal—cause some horrible accident? And above all, would purists and innovators alike recognize and respond to a distinctive style that was a combustive mix of Shakespeare and Chicago?

In his essay, Hulse recounts how risk has been endemic to the *Henry VI* plays from their inception on the Elizabethan stage; but in detailing Hall's effort in the Studio Theater, he illustrates how and why CST has proven willing to embrace such risky endeavors.

When Michael Billington entered Chicago Shakespeare Theater in the summer of 2004, he found that the intimacy of the Courtyard reminded him of the Swan Theater, one of the Royal Shakespeare Company's playing spaces in Stratford. But the aura of familiarity was immediately dispelled by the production he had come to watch:

> what hit me most was the play itself: *King John* directed by Gaines with political urgency so that when Greg Vinkler's king wrapped himself in the flag to justify his military chauvinism, one was reminded less of a medieval English monarch than of George W. Bush. I couldn't quite believe that I was seeing one of Shakespeare's least-loved plays speaking so directly, in the course of a sold-out, ten-week run, to an audience that seemed like a cross-section of Chicago in its mix of middle-class Shakespeare buffs, blue-collar workers, and students.

Building on this experience, Billington, theater critic for *The Guardian*, argues in "In Defense of Ruffled Feathers" for the restoration of the entire Shakespearean canon on contemporary stages and the regular revival of those plays that most directly challenge our modern sensibilities, while noting that this is the standard practice of Chicago Shakespeare Theater, from which, he concludes, the rest of the theatrical world might learn a lesson. The accompanying essays in Part IV of the collection provide examples of these principles at work at CST.

In "'Never did young man fancy': *Troilus and Cressida* and Chicago Shakespeare Theater," Peter Kanelos recalls the three productions of *Troilus and Cressida* that the company has produced in its twenty-five-year history (1987, 1995, and 2007) and recounts how each influenced his own career and work. In fact, the very first play that the company produced in its original home, the Ruth Page Theater, was the very first play of Shakespeare that Kanelos had seen, and the experience proved seminal.

> When the Prologue emerged to introduce the play's action, I was immediately taken with the play. Something was happening in front of me, literally in front of me by a few feet. The drama penetrated the way films never had. This was a singular event, a happening in the here and now. There was something so utterly human, both vulnerable and powerful, that the machine-driven cinema could never replicate. And I was experiencing something quite transformative; not that I knew it then, nor have I ever really considered it until quite recently.

Looking back, Kanelos recounts how a single person, a single theater, and a single play can intersect dynamically over time.

In "At Home with Shakespeare: *Merry Wives* on Stage," Wendy Wall, like Kanelos, demonstrates how scholarship and performance can inform each other. Wall's research focuses on the representation of the domestic sphere on the early modern stage; she found that CST's 2004 production of *Merry Wives of Windsor*, through its design elements and staging, reflected the very themes that were at the center of her own work:

> social tensions come to light—the fraught economics of the marriage market; conflicts over who has the authority to settle local legal matters; class tensions between profligate noblemen and prudent citizens; and concerns about how people of varying national and ethnic backgrounds can unite to form a community. As the play's title insists, these tensions emerge—and are managed— through the lens of domesticity.

After a careful reading of the 2004 production, Wall ultimately concludes that its most profound effect was to make the spectators of the play collaborators in the staging of domesticity.

Michael Shapiro also finds in the productions of CST a prism through which to view subjects central to his own scholarly work. "Two *Merchants*: The Glow of the Roaring Twenties and the Shadow of 9/11" places the two *Merchants of Venice* that the company has staged, in 1997 and 2005, side by side. Shapiro argues that the terror attacks conducted against the United States on September 11, 2001, reverberated in the latter production: "The 1997 production, four years *before* 9/11, encapsulates anti-Semitic 1920s New York, a world characterized by naive frivolity and unaware of the Holocaust to come. The 2005 production, four years *after* the planes hit the Twin Towers and the Pentagon, not only reflects but addresses a world in which ethnic, political, and religious conflicts threaten to engulf us all." Shapiro's essay, in its astute and sensitive comparison of the two *Merchants*, shows us that the boundaries between the stage and the world are porous and ever-shifting.

Yet boundaries *on* stage are also porous and ever-shifting, as Wendy Doniger reminds us in "Gender Blending and Masquerade in *As You Like It* and *Twelfth Night*." Doniger contends, "Gender has a penchant for the theater, and the theater for gender," and, focusing on CST's 2009 *Twelfth Night* and 2011 *As You Like It*, she reads two of Shakespeare's virtuoso gender-contorting performances beside and against each other. Her conclusion is that although gender may be performative, and we can readily recognize its artificiality, we are still subject to its power: "*Twelfth Night* is more fantastic than *As You Like It*, more like *The Tempest*, but both are fantasies, and one should not look too closely at a fantasy. Or, perhaps, we should grant to the characters in the inner frame the same 'double pleasure' and 'conscious illusion' that we grant to ourselves, the right both to see through the trick and to be taken in by it." In the struggle between sober rationality and deeply embedded desires, Doniger suggests, the fantastical, both in life and on the stage, often carries the day.

As is evident from the scope of these collected essays, over its first twenty-five years Chicago Shakespeare Theater has brought new audiences to Shakespeare, invigorated audiences who had become settled in their expectations, provoked reflection, generated debate, and challenged orthodoxies, all while presenting on its stages work that has garnered worldwide acclaim. CST has always remained popular in focus, while insisting that its productions push the edges, aesthetically and conceptually. This compelling combination has served the company well and inspired its artists and its ever-expanding audiences and will most assuredly continue to do so through the next quarter of a century and beyond.

NOTES

1. Sid Smith, "Sounds of the City Fail to Spoil Robust Charm of 'King Henry V,'" *Chicago Tribune*, August 5, 1986.

2. William Shakespeare, *The Life of Henry the Fifth*, ed. Gary Taylor, in *The Oxford Shakespeare*, ed. Stanley Wells and Gary Taylor, 2nd ed. (Oxford: Oxford UP, 2005), Prologue, l.29–31.

3. Gaines won the 1975 Joseph Jefferson Award for best principal actress for her performance in Eugene Ionesco's *The Lesson* for the Orphans Theatre Company and appeared in the world premiere of Marisha Chamberlain's *Scheherazade* at Victory Gardens in 1984 with Aidan Quinn, under the direction of Dennis Zacek. The production earned Victory Gardens its first national honor, the FDG/CBS New Play Award.

4. Qtd. in Richard Christiansen, "'The Prologue and Stage 1, 1986–1990': CST at 20, 1986–2006," *Bill* (Autumn 2005): 17.

5. Barbara Gaines (Artistic Director, Chicago Shakespeare Theater), discussion with the author, July 13, 2011.

6. Ibid.

7. Ibid.

8. Ibid.

9. Ibid.

10. Criss Henderson (Executive Director, Chicago Shakespeare Theater), discussion with the author, December 2, 2011.

11. Gaines, discussion, 2011.

12. Henderson, discussion, 2011. Richard Christiansen is the former chief theater critic at the *Chicago Tribune*.

13. Gaines, discussion, 2011.

14. Henderson, discussion, 2011.

15. Ibid.

16. Gaines, discussion, 2011.

17. See the essays on the "Short Shakespeare!" series by Peter Sagal and Jeffrey Gore in this collection.

18. Beth Charlebois, e-mail message to author, December 7, 2011.

19. Henderson, discussion, 2011.
20. Ibid.; Gaines, discussion, 2011.
21. Henderson, discussion, 2011.
22. Ibid.
23. Ibid.
24. Ibid.

BIBLIOGRAPHY

Christiansen, Richard. "'The Prologue and Stage 1, 1986–1990': CST at 20, 1986–2006." *Bill* (Autumn 2005): 17.

Shakespeare, William. *The Life of Henry the Fifth*. Ed. Gary Taylor. *The Oxford Shakespeare*. Ed. Stanley Wells and Gary Taylor. 2nd ed. Oxford: Oxford UP, 2005.

Smith, Sid. "Sounds of the City Fail to Spoil Robust Charm of 'King Henry V.'" *Chicago Tribune*, August 5, 1986.

PART I

Chicago First

TERRY TEACHOUT

Unlike other Manhattan-based drama critics, I spend almost as much time on the road as I do in New York City. As well as reviewing plays on and off Broadway, I cover regional productions throughout America, and I've learned in the course of my travels that you needn't go to New York, or anywhere near it, to see a first-rate show. Most of this country's theatergoers, alas, don't know that. They reflexively assume that the most important shows are all on Broadway. So did I, until my editor at the *Wall Street Journal* suggested in the winter of 2004 that I might want to see for myself what regional theater was like. Little did I know that I was to become American theater's most frequent flyer, routinely jetting from Massachusetts to Oregon and back again without thinking twice.

It was pure luck that my first stop was Chicago, about whose thriving theater scene I then knew nothing whatsoever. Neither, to be sure, did most New Yorkers: *August: Osage County* had yet to burst upon Broadway in 2004, and my colleagues' awareness of the Chicago stage began and ended with Steppenwolf and the Goodman. The only reason I picked Chicago was that my best friend lived there, and the only reason I picked Chicago Shakespeare Theater was because it was simultaneously mounting a pair of shows—Edward Hall's *Rose Rage* and a revival of *A Little Night Music*—that sounded promising. It never occurred to me when I booked press seats for those two shows that I was about to hit the jackpot, much less that I was destined to return to Chicago's Navy Pier again and again, irresistibly drawn by the work of a company that I have come not merely to esteem but to love.

After my first few visits, I realized that what I was seeing was not just a theater company but a theatrical concept, a modern approach to the classics fully in accord with my own developing sense of what American regional theater at its best is all about. In retrospect, the turning point was Barbara Gaines's 2007 production of *Troilus and Cressida*, to which I responded with the electric enthusiasm that makes a critic's life worth living:

> This is a wartime *Troilus* with a hard political edge—the main set piece is a blood-soaked obelisk reminiscent of the Washington Monument—but Ms. Gaines has taken care not to wear her opinions on her sleeve. Instead, she lets Shakespeare do the talking: "And appetite, an universal wolf, / So doubly seconded with will and power, / Must make perforce an universal prey, / And last eat up himself." You're more than welcome to draw parallels with the war in Iraq if you wish, but it's no less acceptable to approach Ms. Gaines' *Troilus* as a broader parable of man's monstrosity to man. That's where the battle scene comes in. Imagine a dark, empty space filled with mist and lit from below with lurid shafts of light that slice through the fog of war to show us pairs of desperate men locked in mortal combat. You can almost smell the blood—and the fear. . . .
>
> I see a lot of Shakespeare, both in New York and across the country, and the more I see, the more impressed I am by Chicago Shakespeare Theater. Its productions are smart yet accessible, personal yet universal and—above all— consummately theatrical. I can't think of a Shakespeare troupe in America with a higher batting average, and this production of *Troilus and Cressida* will surely be remembered as one of its signal achievements.[1]

That production opened my eyes to the nature of Barbara Gaines's special gift as a director: she is, in the very best sense of the word, a populist, a true believer in the power of the classics to speak directly to contemporary audiences when staged with sharp immediacy and infectious gusto. She is also sure enough of her own talents to make room for equally talented colleagues, and it says much about her generous, enlightened artistic leadership that so many of Chicago Shakespeare's finest productions should be the work of other hands. The best *Follies* I've ever seen, for instance, was the one that Gary Griffin staged there in the fall of 2011 (and how many classical companies, by the way, can claim to do fully as well by Stephen Sondheim as they do by William Shakespeare?).

That said, it is Barbara's shows of which I think first when I think of Chicago Shakespeare, and it is her tough-minded 2005 *Merchant of Venice* that stands out most boldly in my memory.

> Played in modern dress and set in a black-walled rehearsal hall, Ms. Gaines' *Merchant* grapples head-on with the chief problem the play poses for today's audiences, which is that Shakespeare's portrayal of Shylock is widely felt to be openly (if not merely) anti-Semitic. It does so by underlining every reference to Shylock's Jewishness, to the point where the incessant repetition of the word "Jew" shrieks as shrilly as fingernails on a chalkboard. Not that the man himself is spared: Mike Nussbaum plays Shylock as a smug semi-gentleman in a three-piece suit whose elegant cut cannot conceal his raging bloodlust. Yet the more savagely he is treated by the other characters—to the point of being beaten and spat upon in a dark alley—the more intelligible his hateful longings start to seem.[2]

Many Shakespeare productions have moved me, and not a few have thrilled me, but I don't know another one that has *taught* me more about a play I thought I knew well. That, too, is part of Barbara's rich legacy to her fortunate audiences: she is a great teacher whose classroom is the stage. Yet of all the priceless lessons I've learned in the house that Barbara Gaines built, the one I treasure most was the very first one she taught me, which is that great American theater doesn't stop on the banks of the Hudson River. More and more, that's where it starts.

NOTES

1. Terry Teachout, "Tough Nut, Sweet Meat," *Wall Street Journal*, May 18, 2007.
2. Terry Teachout, "Above and Beyond," *Wall Street Journal*, September 30, 2005.

2

Catapulting Shakespeare into the Present
The Artistic Vision of Barbara Gaines

REGINA BUCCOLA

In 1986, Barbara Gaines made a decision that would prove momentous for her, for the Chicago theater community, and for Shakespearean theater worldwide—she decided that Chicago needed a theater devoted to Shakespearean productions. Chicago had a strong tradition of supporting classical arts through institutions such as the Art Institute, the Lyric Opera, and the Chicago Symphony Orchestra, and a clear appetite for more, evinced by the successful relocation of the Joffrey Ballet to Chicago from New York City in 1995. Gaines, however, noticed shortly after her own relocation to Chicago from New York that few Chicago theaters routinely performed Shakespeare plays. Then, as now, Shakespeare appeared in periodic rotation in the seasons of major theaters, such as the Goodman and the Court, or smaller companies, like the Shattered Globe Theatre. Storefront theaters, such as Stage Left, could strategically anchor adventurous theater seasons with Shakespearean plays, audience draws for which the company did not have to pay royalties. But no theater company focused on staging Shakespeare for the Chicago theatergoing audience.

Shakespeare in Chicago seemed a logical choice for Gaines, who finds Shakespeare a playwright that consistently takes the measure of humanity, and Chicago "a human city"; as Gaines declared in a recent interview,

Chicago "is not a cold place. The flesh and blood and nerve endings of the city are very close to the surface; there is a lot of cement in New York City. There is a lot of sky and water and flowers in Chicago—there is less armor to get through."[1] Gaines had found her niche, and she set about filling it.

HUMANIST SHAKESPEARE

During its formative years, the fledgling company, then known as Shakespeare Repertory, presented exclusively Shakespeare's works at the Ruth Page Theater, home to a dance school. Now that the company has been re-christened and taken up residence in its own theater, non-Shakespearean works are often staged, but directors other than Gaines typically oversee these productions. For the twenty-fifth-anniversary season, Gaines shifted gears to direct a non-Shakespearean play (Timothy Findley's *Elizabeth Rex*) featuring Shakespeare as a character. Even when Gaines ventures into other theatrical forms, in other venues, as she did in 2010 with Verdi's *Macbeth* at the Lyric Opera of Chicago, Shakespeare's work has constituted her jumping-off point.

Despite her career-long devotion to Shakespeare's plays, Gaines is not a purist. Discussing her twenty-fifth-anniversary season production of *Timon of Athens*, Gaines bluntly announced: "I've changed the end—I often make a prologue or an epilogue in my productions—no added words, but it's still very powerful."[2] So, for example, the prologue for Gaines's 2009 production of *Richard III* consisted of the central characters of the House of York posing for a family portrait. As an opening bit of stage business, the family portrait provided the audience a crucial visual introduction to many of the significant characters in the devious plots of the title character, upon whose hunched back the entire plot of the play rests. Significantly too, they posed for their portrait on a staircase, with Richard, the heir-aspirant, perched at the very top. Below Richard were assembled the other claimants to the throne, along with his sundry relatives, most of whom would be dead, many by Richard's own machinations, by the play's end.

Gaines's 2004 production of *King John* concluded with a similar gesture: after the slow death spiral of John's disastrous reign ended along with his life, a janitor sauntered onto the stage to remove a defaced poster of King John, replacing it with an image of Prince Henry designed to the exact same specifications, ruefully suggesting that the new regime would, like its promo pieces, mirror the one that preceded it.[3] Even when directing a non-Shakespearean play, such as Timothy Findley's *Elizabeth Rex*, Gaines uses strategically designed prologues to literally set the stage for her production. Gaines cut Findley's frame, set on the night of Shakespeare's death when he recalls the night-long vigil he kept with Elizabeth I prior to the Ash Wednesday 1601 execution of the Earl of Essex. Instead, Gaines's production began with a bit of the final scene of the play Findley imagines the Lord Chamberlain's Men to have performed before Elizabeth on this grim occasion, *Much Ado About Nothing*. Gaines chose to show the Queen watching the final scene, in which Beatrice and Benedict admit their love for each other. Confessions of love loom large in the plot of Findley's play, so this scene prepared the audience for the politically freighted emotional confessions to follow. Such action-based prologues or epilogues to Gaines's productions typically reinforce her interpretation of the text.

David Brailow's review of the 2004 production of *King John* captures another of Gaines's predominant directorial instincts with respect to the structure of Shakespeare's texts: the opportunities they afford for intercutting scenes. When the theater opened on Navy Pier in 1999, Gaines described what a revelation it was to direct in a thrust-stage space, with opportunities for actors to enter from any position upstage, from above, from below, and through the aisles dividing the seating in the main house into three "wedges," one directly downstage, one stage right, and one stage left.[4] It is possible for one huddle of actors to complete their scene upstage right, as another group sweeps into position downstage left and begins their exchange as the upstage actors silently disappear backstage. The pace of the action increases dramatically under such direction, a distinct asset in the tragedies and histories, with plots that often hinge on building and maintaining suspense.

In the case of the 2004 production of *King John*, Gaines not only intercut scenes but also rearranged and layered lines within scenes to suggest the media frenzy of contemporary sound-bite political culture. As David G. Brailow noted in his review:

> 2.1 was framed as a full-fledged political campaign, with King Philip and King John debating at podiums before a fully lit house, the audience standing in for the citizens of Angiers. The speeches of the two Kings were edited and intercut, so that, for example, when France brought Arthur downstage and offered to go home if Angiers accepted him as king, John quickly returned to his podium to interject "Which trust accordingly" into his microphone. As they grew more strident, they spoke simultaneously, each trying to drown the other out.
>
> The Bastard and Constance acted as a contrasting pair to enliven and deconstruct the elaborate show unfolding before us. . . . . Every twist and

7. *King John* (2004) directed by Barbara Gaines, with scenic design by Alexander Dodge. Photo by Liz Lauren

turn of the politicians evoked a sarcastic comment from the Bastard and a passionate response from Constance, rooted in her undisguised ambition and love for her son.[5]

The production thus showcased Gaines's persistent attraction to the seamy underbelly of the political world: the feral teeth behind the saccharine smiles, the manipulation inherent in the rhetorical flourish, the corrupt desire for power over others that taints the claims of desire to serve others.

Although she was a theater major at Northwestern University in Evanston, Illinois, Gaines recalls:

I took some really great political science courses at Northwestern—they were my favorite classes. I am tremendously oversensitive to what happens in the world. It affects me in a way that isn't healthy for me. . . . When I was in Czechoslovakia in 1989, I saw Russian tanks, I saw people—including children—with such sad eyes. I thought of *King John*: "If law can do no right . . .

let it be lawful that law itself is perfect wrong." I did my first *King John* with barbed wire, and Russian words graffitied on the walls.[6]

Gaines's productions thus engage in dialogue with the world around her, representing her impressions of and responses to that world. Asked whether she designs her productions to fit the times or chooses the plays in concert with sociopolitical events from the start, Gaines replies, "Anything can set me off—it can be something in the newspaper, a painting, a dynamic between two people. I am here in the present, and the present catapults me into these shows."[7]

Gaines has tackled with gusto Shakespearean works that are seldom staged, either because they have not been popular with mainstream audiences or because they are perceived as too difficult, complex, or muddled. Gaines's first move, once she decided that Chicago needed a Shakespeare theater, was to mount *Henry V* on the roof of the Red Lion Pub, with rowdy patrons crammed into bleacher seating to watch. A pub-rooftop premiere meant the show was liable to be canceled by the city's notoriously fickle weather, exuberant actors were liable to pitch headlong into a street or alleyway below, and the hard-fought Battle of Agincourt was liable to leave the pub—or Gaines herself—liable for injuries to the patrons, who sometimes witnessed the deaths of soldiers at alarming proximity. *Henry V* is by no means one of Shakespeare's more obscure plays, but neither is it a "standard," like *Hamlet* or *Romeo and Juliet*. In the retrospective conversation that we had about her first quarter century at the helm of Chicago Shakespeare Theater, Gaines recounted going to visit her parents in Florida after *Henry V* closed to wild acclaim. They asked what she planned to do next, recommending "a show that everyone's heard of," instead. Gaines pointed out that she went with "*Troilus and Cressida*, which no one has heard of. One of the reviewers called it 'Toyota and Cressida.' That turned out to be a smart decision, but I didn't do it because it was smart—it's one of my favorite plays. When you're an artist, you follow your soul."[8]

Gaines admits to being a somewhat troubled soul, profoundly moved by the senseless violence, social inequality, and disintegration of community that are fixed features in the modern world. "In many ways I can be a depressive," Gaines muses. "I think the world can be a cruel, dark place, but I think there is warmth in Shakespeare's work, and it can soften us."[9] The operative word in Gaines's assessment is "can." Many of her productions leap directly into the battleground staked out by New Historicist critics of Shakespeare's texts at the end of the twentieth century such as Stephen Greenblatt and Stephen Orgel, who fiercely debated whether the

plays—particularly the histories and "problem plays"—offer subversive social commentary, or whether these plays' theatrical depictions of social sub-
version are meant to serve a cathartic function for viewing audiences.[10] In
such formulations, the play's more turbulent moments are smoothed over
in the memories of the audience by the changing of the guard; the final
speeches of Henry VII in *Richard III* or of Malcolm in *Macbeth* are read as
wake-up calls from the nightmarish chaos the play has explored. However,
those Gainesian epilogues at Chicago Shakespeare Theater typically serve
the function of unsettling the foundations of whatever order has been (re-)
established in the final scene.

So, for instance, the war(s) against terror catapulted Gaines into her 2007
production of *Troilus and Cressida*, which was bookended with stunning
stage pictures that reminded viewers of the soldiers engaged in battle in Iraq
and Afghanistan at the time, as well as soldiers of other times, and other
wars. *Shakespeare Bulletin* reviewer Paul Hecht compellingly described the
production's haunting prologue and epilogue:

> a huge sheet of gauzy fabric billowed out, hanging from the proscenium and
> extending to the end of the platform; fog machines were turned on high, eerie
> music played, and one by one, dead, whitened, stiff warriors strode out of the
> darkness and through the gauze toward the audience, first a trickle, and by the
> end a crowd. That these were soldiers not just from the Trojan War was indi-
> cated by the occasional American WWII-style helmet—war dead of the ages,
> then. That seemed a perfectly weighted reminder of our own current slow-
> burn war, of the ceaseless stream of soldiers sent down into darkness. The play
> ended with the same motif: this time the dead carried out the billowing fabric
> themselves, and covered and enveloped the cursing, coughing Pandarus and,
> as it were, swept the whole play back into oblivion.[11]

Returning to the play with the results of the United States' ill-fated effort to
"shock and awe" Iraq into submission still unfolding inexorably with a daily
accruing body count, Gaines looked at *Troilus and Cressida* anew and saw
even the Greeks' bold siege of Troy, mounted by a vast fleet of a thousand
ships, as an ancient attempt to "shock and awe" the Trojans into returning
the abducted Helen to her husband, which likewise failed miserably, leading
to the appalling destruction of Greeks, of Trojans, of Troy itself. "That's the
other reason to do Shakespeare," Gaines explains. "He is constantly evolving
as you evolve. I've directed some shows three times, but when I go back to
them, I find new things in them, because I'm not the person I was when I
directed it before."[12]

Gaines has returned to *Troilus and Cressida* twice since first offering it to Chicago audiences in 1987. The play came back into favor with theater companies in the early part of the twenty-first century in productions clearly influenced by the Crimean War, World Wars I and II, the Vietnam War, and the Persian Gulf War(s), the wartime resonance of the play clearly providing a reason for its more frequent appearance onstage.[13] The recurrence of war in eastern Europe and the Middle East over the course of the twenty-five years that Gaines has been directing Shakespeare in Chicago has repeatedly driven her back to the cold brutality of *Troilus and Cressida*, in which war heroes are murdered by gangs of vengeful thugs, and women are traded and treated like chattel.

Famously, Shakespeare does not show his audience the Trojan horse, but he does show us Helen; it is a challenge to present onstage the "face that launched a thousand ships" as Shakespeare's theatrical rival Christopher Marlowe put it.[14] Therefore, many directors refuse to even suggest that she is worthy of the attention and, like Barbara Gaines in her 2007 production, depict her as appallingly trashy and cheap, heightening the senseless nature of the conflict.[15] Gaines's 2007 Helen, Mary Kay Cook, subtly channeled a slightly drunken Marilyn Monroe.

Michael Merritt collaborated with Gaines on her 1987 production of *Troilus and Cressida*. Gaines recalled her conversation with Merritt about the stage entrance of Helen. She told him:

> "This is a major moment. Thousands of men were dying during the eleven years of this war for this babe. The moment needs to be sensual and unforgettable." It took Michael all of a few seconds to come up with the idea that to this day people still remember. Across the entire upstage wall of the theatre hung a 20 x 30 foot royal blue scrim. From the distance the audience saw someone take up the bottom of the scrim, a follow spot from upstage hits this blond wild head of hair and perfect body dressed in a white satin gown. She holds the cloth over her head and as she walks downstage it floats down behind her as she carries it towards the audience. Erotic, simple and inexpensive. Theatre at its most dynamic.[16]

Though Gaines now has enviable resources at her disposal for realizing dynamic productions, the early days were much leaner. Gaines considers herself "really lucky—the early designers were so dedicated. They made very little money, as did the actors. Everybody sacrificed so that Chicago could have a Shakespeare Theater."[17]

Paradoxically, the designers who worked on Gaines's 2007 production of *Troilus and Cressida* used their expanded resources to create a war-ravaged set and tattered costumes. Shakespeare's play brings us into the action in medias res, seven years into the war, as the Greek army's morale is sinking and various military leaders in both camps are beginning to absent themselves from battle. The set for Gaines's 2007 production, designed by her frequent collaborator Michael Philippi, conveyed this sense of battle fatigue.[18] The stage floor looked weathered, and it tilted at crazy angles upstage; there was a gigantic, phallic tower stage right, surrounded by scaffolding. Clearly, the war had taken a toll on Troy's infrastructure. The costumes for Helen and Cressida, designed by Nan Cibula-Jenkins, were beautiful, but the fabric was distressed, and soiled around the ankle line. A personification of the physical degradations of war, from trench foot to syphilis, Gaines's Thersites, Ross Lehman, was a creature of rags and patches who seemed to be held together by nothing more than his own sense of outrage and the blood and mucus oozing from the open sores all over his body.

The dynamic that seems to compel Gaines the most is the power dynamic, whether that be the conflict between two rival political powers, the conflict inherent in any attempt to resolve a love triangle into a pair, or power dynamics within relationships that have wider implications, such as Paris's cuckolding of Menelaus. Often, Gaines's production choices telegraph the ways in which centuries of Shakespeare audiences have failed to learn from the plays, highlighting the human tendency to keep making the same mistakes over and over again. In her 2007 production of *Troilus and Cressida*, the titular couple consummated their love on the same bedding used by Paris and Helen. Moreover, Stephen Ouimette's Pandarus voyeuristically ogled both couples, underscoring the common thread in these romances, the savage response these men would have to even the threat of losing "their" woman.

THE WOMAN'S PART

As a feminist performance studies scholar, I often find Gaines's casting and directorial choices to contain powerful, pointed, politicized representations of the female characters, their relationships to the male characters, and their place within the world of the play. Her choices with respect to Cressida and Helen of Troy in 2007's *Troilus and Cressida* offered clear examples of this effect.

Cousin battles cousin in *Troilus and Cressida*, in a conflict that can seem almost arbitrary; when the Trojan Paris—whose theft of Helen occasioned the entire fray—escorts the Greek Diomedes to transfer his brother's beloved

Cressida to the Greeks, he dismisses the sacrifice with: "There is no help: / The bitter disposition of the time / Will have it so," then asks Diomedes, "Who in your thoughts deserves fair Helen best, / Myself or Menelaus?"[19] The shameless hypocrisy inherent in Paris's blithe assertion that the "bitter disposition of the time"—occasioned by his theft of Helen and his refusal to relinquish her to her husband—makes it necessary for his own brother Troilus to surrender *his* beloved to the Greeks was brought to harsh life at Chicago Shakespeare Theater. Diomedes acerbically responded to Paris's comparison of himself and Menelaus, refusing to damn with even the faintest praise, as he witheringly responded: "Both merits poised, each weighs nor less nor more, / But he as he, the heavier for a whore" (4.1.67–68).

No sooner did Gaines's Diomedes (Andrew Rothenberg) take custody of Cressida than he set out to render her a whore as well. The leering Greeks passed Cressida (Chaon Cross) around, heaping lascivious compliments on her as they pawed and fondled her; she was, in essence, gang-raped the moment she entered the Greek camp.[20] Cross played Cressida with compelling nuance, however, leaving ambiguous whether she was a victim of circumstance, who turned to Diomedes for protection in a military camp where she was manhandled from the moment she arrived, or if she was, as Ulysses would have it, a perfect match to Helen in whoredom, as "daughters of the game" (4.6.64). Scholars such as Anthony Dawson have noted the deliberate parallels that Shakespeare constructs between the two women in the play: "both are tokens of war; they each change sides, Helen the Greek is given to [or taken by] a Trojan, Cressida the Trojan is traded to the Greeks. Each takes a new lover in her new environment, though exactly how willingly is not clear. Each is an object of desire, and, precisely because of her desirability, each becomes a 'theme of honour and renown'—an incentive to battle."[21]

Gaines's staging emphasized the interconnections between sexualized politics and politicized sex in the play. Gaines set Cressida's meeting with Diomedes, in which she throws over Troilus for the Greek warrior, on the same mat used in the wrestling match between Ajax and Hector, underscoring the extent to which both encounters feature a Trojan grappling with a Greek. Moreover, Gaines concluded both pairs of meetings on the wrestling mat with an embrace. As Dawson notes, the Greek and Trojan men think that they are fighting "for" women, "over" Helen and Cressida, but notably, the women in the play fight against war. Andromache and Cassandra struggle to prevent Hector from engaging in the battle that both know will prove fatal (5.3.1–93). In his review of the production, Paul Hecht noted the stunning sound effect that accompanied Cassandra's maddened grief in Gaines's production: "a scream in reverse that crescendoed up to an actual scream by

Cassandra."[22] And yet, when asked, in the light of her compelling portrayals of Shakespeare's female characters, if she considers herself a feminist, Gaines demurs, self-identifying instead as a "humanist."[23]

That may be, but the plays to which Gaines has been repeatedly drawn over the course of her career and her productions of them offer much with which feminist Shakespeare scholars such as Wendy Wall, Frances Dolan, and I can grapple. Gaines expresses frank delight that one of the first pieces of theater that some of the thousands of Chicago-area students who attend matinee productions at Chicago Shakespeare Theater each year have ever encountered is *Troilus and Cressida*, and that they have been "completely engaged and overwhelmed" by the force of the play's social critique. "That's the play that I'd like to take to every country and to every world leader," Gaines avers, adding, "I am interested in complexity, problems that can't be solved, the mystery inside of all of us. I've been thinking a lot lately about doing *Measure for Measure* again, and *All's Well*."[24] "Problem plays" like *Troilus and Cressida*, and "problem comedies" like *Measure for Measure* and *All's Well That Ends Well*, with their sordid bed-trick entrapments and queasy depictions of headstrong young men champing at the bit to go to war, are problems with which Gaines enjoys grappling, thereby compelling her audience to grapple.

The signature Gaines prologue and epilogue opened and closed her 2000 production of *All's Well That Ends Well*. The production began with the funeral of Bertram's father, the Count of Roussillon, an event that has already occurred when the action of the play proper begins. The somber opening took its cue from the first scene of Shakespeare's play. In it, the widowed Countess is bidding farewell to her son, who is being sent as a ward to the King of France, and Helena is bidding farewell to the companion of her youth, with whom she has fallen in love, having recently lost her own father. Snow fell softly on the scene; the setting altered over the course of the production to suggest the change of the seasons and the passage of a year. In the production's epilogue, snow fell once again outside of the upstage windows, as the assembled courtiers waltzed. In a moment reminiscent of the final wistful scene in *The Graduate*, when Benjamin Braddock (Dustin Hoffman) and Elaine Robinson (Katharine Ross) sit mutely in growing consternation in the rear of a bus after jubilantly fleeing her marriage to another man, the reunited Bertram and Helena whirled through a ballroom full of joyful dancers to a standstill center stage, looking at each other, silently taking the full measure of all that had passed between them already and the long road that stretched ahead of them.

Chicago theater critic Lawrence Bommer described *All's Well That Ends Well*, which rounded out the inaugural season on Navy Pier, as an "alleged comedy" and "a misanthropic fairy tale"; however, he found that Gaines's

8. Cast of *All's Well that Ends Well* (2000), with Bertram (Timothy Gregory) kneeling before a visibly pregnant Helena (Lia D. Mortensen), directed by Barbara Gaines. Photo by Michael Brosilow

"redemptive staging recalls Francois Truffaut's *The Story of Adele H*, another tale of a haunted woman who lost her heart (and mind) to an unregenerate soldier. Somehow this production makes Helena's misery matter."[25] In discussing the play, Gaines conveyed her sense both of the way that the male-dominated world depicted in the play circumscribes the choices of Helena and the other female characters and of the ways in which Helena's choices prove deleterious for her. "Women have no power at all in the world of this play," Gaines noted. "The fact that women take control over the bed trick as a response to male dominance is, for me, not a bad thing. . . . I like the way Shakespeare uses the convention [the bed trick], both in this play and in *Measure for Measure*, because his women find a way to expose the males' duplicity. But to be entirely fair, the women have been duplicitous, too."[26]

Gaines's keen interest in the complexity of the female characters in another of her favorite plays, *Measure for Measure*, was readily apparent to reviewers of her 2005 production. Writing for the *Shakespeare Bulletin*, Harvey Young noted:

Contrary to expectations, the brothel scene helped to maintain the theme of female independence that Gaines consistently developed throughout the play. The onstage prostitutes, who performed a series of simulated sex acts and repeatedly yawned throughout each of them, gave the impression that they did not derive any enjoyment from their job. This was work, nothing more. Mistress Overdone was big and bawdy. In her interactions with assembled audience members, she repeatedly bullied married men—urging them to leave their wives and to select a prostitute of their choosing. Over and over again, the embarrassed spectators, stunned into silence, would wait powerlessly until Mistress Overdone decided to move on to another victim. In the other scenes, this theme of female independence chiefly appeared in Dana Green's characterization of Isabella as a brash, powerful, and self-involved woman.[27]

Emphasizing Isabella's self-possession and verve certainly bolsters the critique of patriarchal hegemony in *Measure for Measure*, which divides its settings among a prison visited by a faux friar, the world of the brothel, and the world of a corrupt court where sexual negotiations worthy of the brothel are falsely promised as a get-out-of-jail-free card.

Significantly, the lone comedy not classed as a "problem play" that keeps Gaines coming back for more is *The Merry Wives of Windsor*, the only Shakespearean comedy that foregrounds and celebrates its female characters from the title straight through to Act 5. Gaines recounts: "One day, Michael Boyd, Artistic Director at the Royal Shakespeare Company, was here and we were talking about shows that we liked, and he asked if I do any comedies. I said that I hoped I matured enough to be able to do the comedies. One of my favorite plays is one that most people like the least—*Merry Wives of Windsor*—because it's about community."[28] Specifically, *The Merry Wives of Windsor* is about a community with women at its heart—the witty and wise merry wives of the title responsible for the maintenance of social and marital order; the gossipy governess of domestic affairs, Mistress Quickly; and the self-actualized Anne Page, who forges her own path into her own future family.[29]

However, it is not only instances in which Gaines depicts female characters as "brash" and "powerful" that call attention to her directorial vision of them; sometimes it is her decision to depict them at all. Consider Gaines's *Richard III*, the first play of the 2009–2010 season. Writing during the reign of a powerful female monarch, Elizabeth I, Shakespeare, significantly, placed a trio of women at the center of his version of a well-known story of bloody civil conflict based in political competition that could just as easily have been a testosterone-fest. These three women are Margaret of

9. Felicia P. Fields and Kevin Gudahl in *Measure for Measure* (2005), directed by Barbara Gaines. Photo by Liz Lauren

Anjou, the widowed queen of Henry VI; Queen Elizabeth, almost immediately widowed herself when King Edward IV dies in the play's second act; and Queen Anne, widowed in the action of *3 Henry VI* before she could become the Lancastrian queen of Henry's son, Edward. Dismissed by Richard as a "foul wrinkled witch" (*Richard III*, 1.3.164), Margaret was played in Gaines's production by Jennifer Harmon as a wild-haired, white-faced embodiment of collateral damage. Costume designer Susan Mickey placed Margaret in tattered clothing that served to remind the audience that the banished former queen was, effectively, a homeless woman. Mickey delivered her first lines standing in the center aisle of the main floor seating in a voice as ragged as her clothes, a monarchal Miss Havisham frozen at the moment she lost king/husband, prince/son, and kingdom.

Margaret serves as a sort of Chorus figure, who keeps reminding the audience of what has happened, and foretelling events to come.[30] The authority with which Margaret delivers horrific prophecies that come inexorably true links her to the spirit world that plays a prominent role in Shakespeare's play, as it did in Gaines's production, which was repeatedly haunted by ghosts of the recently dead.[31] Gaines said of the women in the play:

> Even though not one of them is flawless, the women are, for me, the soul of the play. They are the observers and the witnesses of carnage. Their entire lives have been lived through the lens of this hundred-year war—and it has made them tough. They are articulate and, in some ways, fearless—and they are tied together by their hatred for Richard. Because they have no political power, the women are afforded a wisdom and see things that the men do not. It is the women who witness and acknowledge that violence begets more violence, generation after generation.[32]

And yet, these very women are often cut from productions, a trend that began in the eighteenth century, with the tender revisionary ministrations of the celebrated Shakespearean impresarios David Garrick and Colley Cibber. Cibber cut Margaret entirely, an impulse followed centuries later by Laurence Olivier in a 1944 theatrical production of *Richard III* famously reprised ten years later in his third Shakespearean film.

Predictably, perhaps, Olivier sharply cut the women's roles in order to focus attention on Richard himself, whom he portrayed; thus, he eliminated Margaret entirely, and Anne's and the Duchess of York's lines were severely curtailed. Richard Loncraine took the same course a half century later in his mid-1990s film version of *Richard III*, which envisions Richard as a fascist sporting a Hitler mustache, whose speech accepting the mantle of king is suggestive of the Nuremberg rally. No Margaret once again, though some of her more spectacular curses of Richard were put in the mouth of Annette Bening, as Queen Elizabeth.[33] Historically, Margaret was not present in the Yorkist court of Edward IV and Richard III; Shakespeare's decision to place her anachronistically there in the role of Cursemaster General compellingly complicates the male dominance of the royal line during the Wars of the Roses, a complexity fruitfully explored in Gaines's production.

THE CHICAGO SHAKESPEARE THEATER COMMUNITY

When Gaines says of Shakespeare, "He's the closest thing to life itself that humanity has; most of us spend our lives trying to figure out who we are and what it's all about, and Shakespeare is the greatest single source of human understanding that we have—what your own humanity, personally, can mean to you," one could be forgiven for hearing echoes of Harold Bloom. In the prologue to his book that made the audacious titular claim that Shakespeare invented the human, Bloom opined, "Bardolatry, the worship of Shakespeare, ought to be even more a secular religion than it already is. The plays remain the outward limit of human achievement: aesthetically, cognitively, in certain ways morally, even spiritually. . . . Shakespeare will go on explaining us, in part because he invented us."[34] While Gaines may not agree that Shakespeare invented the species in all of its existential, introspective glory, she certainly sees the plays as explorations of what it means to be human.

However, Gaines's long relationship with Shakespeare has not rendered her a Bardolator. Speaking of Timothy Findley's depiction of Shakespeare in *Elizabeth Rex*, Gaines said, "I love what he [Findley] did with Shakespeare. He's just a cranky, annoyed writer and producer. He's so real; in some ways, so ordinary, and I like that because Shakespeare was a man."[35] Sounding her common theme, Gaines is drawn to the humanity of Shakespeare, as she is drawn to the humanity of the characters he created.

Economic imperatives might drive a Shakespeare theater situated next to a Ferris wheel on a former naval installation that is currently one of the Second City's major tourist attractions to steer a steady course for popular, palatable Shakespeare in the main house, where ticket sales are the stuff of life: a superabundance of Ariels and Pucks and Romeos and Juliets. Criss Henderson and Barbara Gaines have eschewed such an approach. As David G. Brailow noted of the 2004 season:

> Patrons of Chicago Shakespeare Theater had a unique opportunity in the
> 2003–04 season to see four of the least often performed history plays—the

three parts of *Henry VI* in *Rose Rage* and *King John*. They were also treated to widely divergent presentational and interpretive styles. *Rose Rage* depicted the English political world as a meat locker trapping its denizens in a gory cycle of brief triumph and death. But *King John*, despite its caustic treatment of power politics, became an intensely emotional portrayal of deeply flawed human beings trying as best they could to find their way "among the thorns and dangers of this world." The tightly focused, lucid direction and performances laid bare the characters' struggles between self-interest and conscience.[36]

The 2004 season's offering of *King John* on the main stage, and *Rose Rage* in the upstairs "black box" studio space, offers a prime example of the dialogic dynamic among the productions onstage at Chicago Shakespeare Theater over the course of a season, enabled by the upstairs/downstairs structure of the theater.

Like Shakespeare himself, Gaines began her career in theater as an actor but has had her greatest success as a stakeholder in a theater company. Also like Shakespeare, she has a cohort of loyal actors around whom she can build her concepts for shows, many of whom have appeared in numerous productions, progressing from youthful roles to mature ones. Chicago Shakespeare Theater stalwart Larry Yando began his career with the theater as Hortensio in the 1993–1994 production of *Shrew*, took on the role of Henry IV in 1999, and has recently played Malvolio (in Rourke's production of *Twelfth Night* in 2009), among numerous other roles. Like many actors who have portrayed Celia in *As You Like It* only to "graduate" to the role of Rosalind, Kate Fry, who garnered rave reviews for her performance as Rosalind/Ganymede in Gary Griffin's 2011 production, cut her teeth in the play as David Bell's Celia in his 2001 production for Chicago Shakespeare Theater. Kevin Gudahl has appeared in numerous Chicago Shakespeare Theater productions over the years, including as William Shakespeare himself in the 2011 production of *Elizabeth Rex*, and like many of the theater's "regulars," he is also a familiar face in Shakespearean productions at other prestigious Chicago theaters; he appeared in *Othello* at the Writers' Theatre and in *Titus Andronicus* at the Court Theatre and served as the loyal Albany to Stacy Keach's *King Lear* at the Goodman.

"Chicago is a city a talented actor can make a life in and work regularly in," Executive Director Criss Henderson noted. "Our actors were excellent to begin with, but now many of them have twenty-five years of experience—they can get their heads and mouths around the language regularly. That is certainly part of the muscularity with which we are able to stage these plays."[37]

Without actors, there is no theater. In recognition of the fact that the new theater belonged to them, the lone time that the thrust stage at Chicago

Shakespeare Theater has been used in a conventional proscenium manner was the first day that the actors got to see it. They were ushered into the backstage area where they assembled, champagne in hand, before a vast fire curtain. Once all were present and accounted for, the curtain rose to unveil the thrust stage, the gallery seating, the theater. Their theater.

Some members of the Chicago Shakespeare Theater community have completed an apprenticeship with the theater before going on to pursue other endeavors. They have a tendency, however, to return "home" to the theater. Sean Graney, for example, worked as Chicago Shakespeare Theater's house manager when they were based at the Ruth Page Theater, shortly after he finished college. He went on to start the wildly successful Hypocrites Theater Company. A wunderkind director, Graney made a triumphant return to Chicago Shakespeare Theater in 2008 to direct Christopher Marlowe's *Edward II* in a promenade staging for the upstairs studio theater, which Andrea Stevens characterized as "simply put, one of the most exciting performances I've recently seen" in her review for *Shakespeare Bulletin.*[38]

When asked what has surprised her the most over the course of her twenty-five years building and nurturing Chicago Shakespeare Theater, Gaines replies, "How beloved the theater has become has been the most surprising,"[39] referring not only to the theater's loyal audience and patron base but also to the small army of creative and administrative staff that has signed up to serve under Gaines's command:

> We have an amazing staff that is just so dedicated. People are passionate about their work—it's inspiring; I understand why I'm inspired, but it's touching to see the eighty other people who work here that passionate, every day. And the level of the talent grows every year. Just when you think it can't get any better, it takes a huge step forward; Gary Griffin, Rick Boynton, Bob Mason—they are great collaborators; trust me, we would never have gotten as far without them.[40]
>
> Deb Acker—our Stage Manager since 1990; Lisa Stec—one of the greatest drapers; Dan Hess, who started out as House Manager and now he's Company Manager; Chris Plevin has just turned thirty and he's Director of Productions; it's a job for a fifty-year-old—he's astounding. They are really proud of the work that we do—their hearts are in it. I couldn't have imagined that. I didn't know anything, other than that Shakespeare needed to be done. We've created a community, Gaines marvels; I had no idea that I would be creating a community.[41]

Marilyn Halperin, Director of Education and Communications, points out that a community is precisely what is created at the end of Gaines's favorite comedy, *The Merry Wives of Windsor*. The cuckold-phobe, Ford, makes amends with his long-suffering loyal wife; the Pages reconcile for their abortive efforts to outwit one another as matchmakers for their daughter and resign themselves to her own choice of husband; Falstaff is punished for his treble efforts to disrupt marital harmony with his lecherous, adulterous advances and is then reintegrated into the Windsor community. All of this is accomplished under the wise and witty leadership of the Windsor wives, Mistress Ford and Mistress Page, who script, direct, and stage manage the play's increasingly elaborate metatheatrical deceptions. Little wonder that Barbara Gaines has been repeatedly drawn to this play—like the Windsor wives, she is in the business of making theater that is equal parts myth, magic, and moral message.

NOTES

1. Barbara Gaines (Artistic Director, Chicago Shakespeare Theater), discussion with the author, July 13, 2011.

2. Ibid.

3. For a full discussion of this production, see David G. Brailow, "*King John,*" *Shakespeare Bulletin* 22.2 (2004): 90–95, accessed August 8, 2011, *Academic OneFile*.

4. Barbara Gaines, discussion with the author, Chicago Shakespeare Theater, October 1999. While the stage at the Ruth Page Theater offered a shallow thrust design, the stage at Chicago Shakespeare Theater extends much farther into the audience. For more on the relationship between the theater's design and the productions mounted within it, see Jonathan Walker's essay in this volume.

5. Brailow, "*King John,*" 92.

6. Gaines, discussion, 2011.

7. Ibid.

8. Ibid. While Chicago audiences (and reviewers) may have thought "Toyota" when they heard "Cressida" in 1987, Anthony B. Dawson notes that, since the 1960s and 1970s, when *Troilus and Cressida* "came into its own as an anti-war play . . . it has become a standard in the repertoire, performed almost as often as *Hamlet* or *As You Like It* in theatres in England and North America." See Anthony B. Dawson, ed., introduction to *Troilus and Cressida*, by William Shakespeare, *The New Cambridge Shakespeare*, ed. Brian Gibbons (Cambridge: Cambridge UP, 2003), 50. Nevertheless, Gretchen Minton was still able to recall in 2008 that "as an undergraduate student, I was part of a ten-person performance group within my Shakespeare class; our daunting task was to produce a portion of the strangest and most difficult play we had read all year: *Troilus and Cressida,*" ultimately referring to it as "this odd play that none of us had even heard of before." Minton later mused over Toyota's injudicious choice of "Cressida" as a car model name: "Why would anyone buy a car that is destined to be unfaithful?" See Gretchen E. Minton, "'Discharging less than the tenth part of one': Performance Anxiety and/in *Troilus and Cressida,*" in *Shakespeare and the Cultures of Performance*, ed. Paul Yachnin and Patricia Badir (Burlington, VT: Ashgate, 2008), 101 and 114, n. 32.

9. Gaines, discussion, 2011.

10. For one of the clearest articulations of the subversion/containment model, see Stephen Greenblatt, *Shakespearean Negotiations* (Berkeley and Los Angeles: U of California P, 1988). For a few foundational articulations of New Historicist theoretical constructs, see Catherine Gallagher and Stephen Greenblatt, "Introduction," in *Practicing New Historicism* (Chicago: U of Chicago P, 2000), 1–19; Lisa Jardine, "Introduction," *Reading Shakespeare Historically* (New York: Routledge, 1996), 1–18; David Scott Kastan, *Shakespeare after Theory* (New York: Routledge, 1999); and *New Historicism and Renaissance Drama*, ed. and intro. Richard Wilson and Richard Dutton, Longman Critical Readers, ed. Raman Selden and Stan Smith (New York: Longman, 1992). For more recent critical response to the formulations of New Historicism, see Jürgen Pieters, "Critical Self-Fashioning: Stephen Greenblatt and the New Historicism: General Introduction," in *Critical Self-Fashioning: Stephen Greenblatt and The New Historicism* (New York: Peter Lang, 1999), 11–20; and Douglas Bruster, *Shakespeare and the Question of Culture: Early Modern Literature and the Cultural Turn*, Early Modern Cultural Series, ed. Ivo Kamps (New York: Palgrave Macmillan, 2003), particularly the preface, xv–xxi.

11. Paul Hecht, "Shakespeare in Chicagoland," *Shakespeare Bulletin* 26.2 (2008): 201–11, accessed August 8, 2011, *Academic OneFile*; the quoted passage appears on page 205. As Peter Holland notes, such an approach must be carefully calibrated, to avoid

> the lure of the analogue, the precise historical analogy that would serve to illuminate the whole, relying on our knowledge of more recent history to explicate the Shakespearian text as if the play had no function in relation to its own time and, more significantly, could only be made popular by the recreation of the play as modern parable . . . at its worst . . . trying to make Shakespeare popular makes the productions weakly populist, offering simple answers where the text is complex, failing to follow through the implications of analogy.

See Peter Holland, "Shakespeare Performances in England, 1990–1," *Shakespeare Survey: An Annual Survey of Studies and Production* 45 (1993): 115–44; the quoted passage appears on page 130.

12. Gaines, discussion, 2011.

13. See Dawson's overview of this trend in *Troilus and Cressida*, 50–52.

14. Christopher Marlowe, *Doctor Faustus*, in *The Complete Plays*, ed. J. B. Steane (London: Penguin Books, 1986), 5.1.97–98.

15. Sam Mendes took a similar approach with his Helen (Sally Dexter) at the Royal Shakespeare Company in 1990. Helen made her initial stage entrance on a plinth draped with gold lamé; the drape covered her entirely, making her resemble, curiously, a pyramid. When the drape was whipped away to reveal her to the Greeks and to the theater audience, they were treated to a garish vision in heavy make-up, with particular emphasis on her pouty, shiny, cherry-red lips.

16. "About Michael Merritt," The Merritt Award for Excellence in Design and Collaboration, accessed August 8, 2011.

17. Gaines, discussion, 2011.

18. Philippi died suddenly in Chicago in 2009, while working with another of his frequent collaborators, the Goodman Theatre's Robert Falls, on *High Holidays*. Chris Jones, "Michael Philippi, Major Chicago Lighting Designer, Dies," *Chicago Tribune*, The Theater Loop, October 27, 2009.

19. William Shakespeare, *Troilus and Cressida*, ed. Gary Taylor, in *The Oxford Shakespeare: The Complete Works*, 2nd ed., ed. Stanley Wells and Gary Taylor (Oxford UP, 2005), 4.1.48–50 and 55–56. Subsequent references to the plays will be to this edition and will be parenthetically cited in the text. Anthony Dawson notes "the intermingled blood and desire that underpin the whole conflict, which is in many respects a civil war." See Dawson, ed., *Troilus and Cressida*, 15 and also 63.

20. As Dawson notes in offering a production history of *Troilus and Cressida*, such an interpretation of Cressida's arrival in the Greek camp is not uncommon. See Dawson, ed., *Troilus and Cressida*, 55–59 and 62. Minton notes that Cressida's reception in the Greek camp is of a piece with her treatment elsewhere in the play, since Pandarus and Troilus collude to "tease Cressida the morning after [her sexual liaison with Troilus], making jokes about her anatomy—a sort of locker-room banter with her present. The near gang rape that she experiences at the hands of the Greek soldiers is a horrific extension of how she has already been treated by her lover and uncle." See Minton, "'Discharging less than the tenth part of one,'" 106.

21. Dawson, ed., *Troilus and Cressida*, 15.

22. Hecht, "Shakespeare in Chicagoland," 205.

23. Gaines, discussion, 2011.

24. Ibid.

25. Lawrence Bommer, "*All's Well That Ends Well*," *Chicago Reader*, May 4, 2000.

26. Marilyn Halperin and Gina Buccola, "A Conversation with Director Barbara Gaines," All's Well That Ends Well *Teacher Handbook*, Chicago Shakespeare Theater, 2000.

27. Harvey Young, "*Measure for Measure*," *Shakespeare Bulletin* 23.3 (2005): 115–17, accessed August 8, 2011, *Academic OneFile*; the quoted passage appears on page 116.

28. Gaines, discussion, 2011.

29. For feminist analyses of *Merry Wives*, see Sandra Clark, "'Wives may be merry and yet honest too': Women and Wit in *The Merry Wives of Windsor* and Some Other Plays," in "*Fanned and Winnowed Opinions*": Shakespearean Essays Presented to Harold Jenkins, ed. John W. Mahon and Thomas A. Pendleton (New York: Methuen, 1987), 249–67; Carol Thomas Neely, "Constructing Female Sexuality in the Renaissance: Stratford, London, Windsor, Vienna," in *Feminism and Psychoanalysis*, ed. Richard Feldstein and Judith Roof (Ithaca, NY: Cornell UP, 1989), 209–29; and Wendy Wall, "Why Does Puck Sweep? Fairylore, Merry Wives, and Social Struggle," *Shakespeare Quarterly* 52.1 (2001): 67–106.

30. See also Marie-Hélène Besnault and Michel Bitot, "Historical Legacy and Fiction: The Poetical Reinvention of King Richard III," in *The Cambridge Companion to Shakespeare's History Plays*, ed. Michael Hattaway (Cambridge: Cambridge UP, 2002), 119.

31. In her interview for the play's program, Barbara Gaines told Director of Education and Communication, Marilyn Halperin: "Peter Brook once said that if you don't believe in the spirit world, then you really needn't bother to open these plays, because for Shakespeare the spirits are real and palpable. For me, the spirit world is connected to our collective unconscious and, like our dreams, is truthful. It is a world that we are inclined to push away, that we wish not to deal with. Shared by all humankind, past and present, I see it as a great undertow that connects us to one another." Barbara Gaines and Marilyn Halperin, "The Undertow of *Richard III*: Director Q&A," *Richard III Playbill* (Autumn 2009): 12.

32. Ibid., 11.

33. *King Richard III*, dir. Laurence Olivier, perf. Laurence Olivier, John Gielgud, and Claire Bloom (London Film Productions, 1955) and *Richard III*, dir. Richard Loncraine, perf. Ian McKellen, Annette Bening, Kristin Scott Thomas, John Wood, and Maggie Smith (Mayfair Entertainment International, 1995).

34. Harold Bloom, "To the Reader," in *Shakespeare: The Invention of the Human* (New York: Riverhead Books, 1998), xix–xx.

35. Gaines, discussion, 2011.

36. Brailow, "*King John*," 90–91.

37. Criss Henderson (Executive Director, Chicago Shakespeare Theater), discussion with the author, December 2, 2011.

38. Andrea Stevens, "Edward II," *Shakespeare Bulletin* 27.1 (2009): 117–22, accessed August 8, 2011, *Academic OneFile*; the quoted passage appears on page 117.

39. Gaines, discussion, 2011.

40. Gary Griffin is the Associate Artistic Director, Rick Boynton is the Creative Producer, and Bob Mason is Artistic Associate/Casting Director.

41. Gaines, discussion, 2011.

BIBLIOGRAPHY

"About Michael Merritt." The Merritt Award for Excellence in Design and Collaboration. Accessed August 8, 2011.

Besnault, Marie-Hélène, and Michel Bitot. "Historical Legacy and Fiction: The Poetical Reinvention of King Richard III." *The Cambridge Companion to Shakespeare's History Plays*. Ed. Michael Hattaway, 106–25. Cambridge: Cambridge UP, 2002.

Bloom, Harold. *Shakespeare: The Invention of the Human*. New York: Riverhead Books, 1998.

Bommer, Lawrence. "*All's Well That Ends Well*." *Chicago Reader*. May 4, 2000.

Brailow, David G. "*King John*." *Shakespeare Bulletin* 22.2 (2004): 90–95. Accessed August 8, 2011. *Academic OneFile*.

Bruster, Douglas. *Shakespeare and the Question of Culture: Early Modern Literature and the Cultural Turn*. Early Modern Cultural Series. Ed. Ivo Kamps. New York: Palgrave Macmillan, 2003.

Clark, Sandra. "'Wives may be merry and yet honest too': Women and Wit in *The Merry Wives of Windsor* and Some Other Plays." *"Fanned and Winnowed Opinions": Shakespearean Essays Presented to Harold Jenkins*. Ed. John W. Mahon and Thomas A. Pendleton, 249–67. New York: Methuen, 1987.

Dawson, Anthony B., ed. "Introduction." *Troilus and Cressida*. By William Shakespeare. The New Cambridge Shakespeare. Ed. Brian Gibbons. Cambridge: Cambridge UP, 2003.

Gaines, Barbara, and Marilyn Halperin. "The Undertow of *Richard III*: Director Q&A." *Richard III* (Chicago Shakespeare Theater, Autumn 2009): 10–12.

Gallagher, Catherine, and Stephen Greenblatt. *Practicing New Historicism*. Chicago: U of Chicago P, 2000.

Greenblatt, Stephen. *Shakespearean Negotiations*. Berkeley and Los Angeles: U of California P, 1988.

Halperin, Marilyn, and Gina Buccola. "A Conversation with Director Barbara Gaines." All's

Well That Ends Well *Teacher Handbook*. Chicago: Chicago Shakespeare Theater, 2000.

Hecht, Paul. "Shakespeare in Chicagoland." *Shakespeare Bulletin* 26.2 (2008): 201–11. Accessed August 8, 2011. *Academic OneFile*.

Holland, Peter. "Shakespeare Performances in England, 1990–1." *Shakespeare Survey: An Annual Survey of Studies and Production* 45 (1993): 115–44.

Jardine, Lisa. "Introduction." *Reading Shakespeare Historically*. New York: Routledge, 1996. 1–18.

Jones, Chris. "Michael Philippi, Major Chicago Lighting Designer, Dies." *Chicago Tribune*. The Theater Loop. October 27 2009.

Kastan, David Scott. *Shakespeare after Theory*. New York: Routledge, 1999.

King Richard III. Dir. Laurence Olivier. Perf. Laurence Olivier, John Gielgud, and Claire Bloom. London Film Productions, 1955.

Marlowe, Christopher. *Doctor Faustus*. *The Complete Plays*. Ed. J. B. Steane. London: Penguin Books, 1986.

Minton, Gretchen E. "'Discharging less than the tenth part of one': Performance Anxiety and/in *Troilus and Cressida*." *Shakespeare and the Cultures of Performance*. Ed. Paul Yachnin and Patricia Badir, 101–19. Burlington, VT: Ashgate, 2008.

Neely, Carol Thomas. "Constructing Female Sexuality in the Renaissance: Stratford, London, Windsor, Vienna." *Feminism and Psychoanalysis*. Ed. Richard Feldstein and Judith Roof, 209–29. Ithaca, NY: Cornell UP, 1989.

New Historicism and Renaissance Drama. Ed. and introduced by Richard Wilson and Richard Dutton. Longman Critical Readers. Ed. Raman Selden and Stan Smith. New York: Longman, 1992.

Pieters, Jürgen. *Critical Self-Fashioning: Stephen Greenblatt and The New Historicism*. New York: Peter Lang, 1999.

Richard III. Dir. Richard Loncraine. Perf. Ian McKellen, Annette Bening, Kristin Scott Thomas, John Wood, and Maggie Smith. Mayfair Entertainment International, 1995.

Shakespeare, William. *Troilus and Cressida*. Ed. Gary Taylor. *The Oxford Shakespeare: The Complete Works*. Ed. Stanley Wells and Gary Taylor. 2nd ed. Oxford UP, 2005.

Stevens, Andrea. "*Edward II.*" *Shakespeare Bulletin* 27.1 (2009): 117–22. Accessed August 8, 2011. *Academic OneFile*.

Wall, Wendy. "Why Does Puck Sweep? Fairylore, Merry Wives, and Social Struggle." *Shakespeare Quarterly* 52.1 (2001): 67–106.

Young, Harvey. "*Measure for Measure.*" *Shakespeare Bulletin* 23.3 (2005): 115–17. Accessed August 8, 2011. *Academic OneFile*.

Barbara, Shakespeare, and Me

JONATHAN ABARBANEL

Chicago Shakespeare Theater? Sure, I can tell you how I started that. Have a seat.

Barbara Gaines and I met as Cherubs the summer we were seventeen. We were attending the National High School Institute at Northwestern University in Evanston, Illinois, a program for precocious high-schoolers between their junior and senior years, nicknamed "The Cherubs" since Time Immemorial. We weren't the only Cherubs that summer to become rich and famous: the successful actors Joe Bratcher and Davis Hall were among our number, as well as little Bobby Reich, a charismatic overachiever who went on to pursue a doctorate in economics and become Secretary of Labor under President Bill Clinton.

The times being what they were—this was about forty-five years ago—the concept of in loco parentis was in full force, which meant that boys and girls were housed in separate dormitories at the extreme opposite ends of the campus, about a mile apart. There would be no casual familiarity in this happy camp (and it *was* a happy camp because we knew we were the brightest and the best, and we were having a wonderful time) and no private intimacies on the nearby beaches of the Lake Michigan shoreline. To hammer the nail into the coffin of adolescent libido, our dormitory cafeteria food was liberally laced with saltpeter—no disguising that unsavory taste—leading to much-discussed frustration among the boys. You'll have to ask Barbara how the girls reacted to it. Or maybe they thought only boys needed to be dosed.

In addition to classes in acting, costume design, and scenic design, each acting Cherub was in an end-of-summer show, fully mounted in the then splendid (and now sadly outdated) Cahn Auditorium, at that time the main theater venue on the Northwestern campus. There were four or five shows, as I recall, each one running between forty and ninety minutes. One of the staff directors did *The Apollo of Belloc*, and there also were productions of act 1 of the musical *Archy and Mehitabel*, a condensed *Romeo and Juliet*, and then the project that Barbara and I were in, a condensed staging of Turgenev's *A Month in the Country*. We must'a been the brightest and the best, because our directors were throwing some serious stuff at us. At seventeen, I barely knew who Chekhov was and had not yet read any of his plays, let alone his less-famous, heavy-duty precursor Turgenev. Hey, I'd never even acted in a classical play of any kind, unless you count a drama club reading of *The Importance of Being Earnest*. And here Barbara and I were in made-to-measure period costumes (another first for me as an actor), performing on scenery created just for us and receiving a crash course in Russian tea drinking, samovar protocol, and mid-nineteenth-century Slavic society.

More to the point, Barbara and I played opposite each other in *A Month in the Country*, I as Dr. Shpigelsky and Barbara as Lizaveta, the governess-companion in the wealthy household in which the play is set. Both were supporting roles, but not insubstantial ones, and we had a flirtatious scene together that included dancing. Somewhere, in someone's trunk (perhaps mine), there is a photo of us *en scène*. At the final celebratory dinner, which ended our intense five weeks as Cherubs, Barbara and I vowed to reunite "in ten years on Broadway together."

I went on to attend Tufts University and then, sponsored by Tufts, lived in London where I studied with playwright James Forsyth, eminent directors E. Martin Brown and Anthony Cornish, theater architect Victor Glasstone, and poet George Macbeth, among others. Curiously, in all my studies at home and abroad, I never performed Shakespeare. My classical acting efforts included Jacobean revenge tragedy, Restoration comedy, Molière, and medieval mystery cycle plays. But I saw—live, and more than once—the great actors of the older generation such as Laurence Olivier, John Gielgud, Ian Richardson, and Edith Evans, and those of the mid-generation such as Paul Scofield, Alec Guinness, Flora Robson, and Donald Sinden, and those of the new generation such as Derek Jacobi, Jeremy Brett, Judi Dench, and Frances de la Tour. I inhaled the work of directors such as Peter Brook, Peter Hall, Clifford Williams, and Trevor Nunn, as well as then-new playwrights such as Tom Stoppard and Simon Gray. I also bought a peacock's wardrobe of mod clothes on the King's Road, but that's another story.

Barbara enrolled at Northwestern (which used the Cherubs as a recruitment tool), where she came under the life-altering professorship and mentorship of Dr. Wallace Bacon. She then went on to New York, where she spent a decade or so doing I-don't-know-what before returning to Chicago, where she had theater friends, Northwestern friends, and —obviously—ambitions.

Barbara and I had our roughly ten-year reunion in 1975, but it wasn't on Broadway; it was at Orphans Pub on Lincoln Avenue in Chicago, in a then-radical-chic neighborhood that was the epicenter of the Off-Loop Theater Movement in its first flower. Just down the street from Orphans were The Body Politic (home to Paul Sills's Story Theatre and Stuart Gordon's Organic Theater Company) and Kingston Mines Theater Company (where *Grease* was created). I worked as an actor and a director at both houses for little to no pay at a time when few Off-Loop venues were under Equity contracts. Barbara, who had earned her Equity card in New York, received a tiny bit more at Orphans, where the owner had turned the back room into a pub theater. Barbara was there performing in Ionesco's *The Lesson*. It ran just a few weeks but was a surprising Off-Loop hit for which Barbara received the first of many Joseph Jefferson Awards, her only Jeff Award for acting (although she was nominated one other time).

We saw each other at widely spaced intervals over the next several years, usually briefly backstage when I saw her in a show or at the odd party or two. I gradually moved out of acting and into theater criticism (initially for underground papers) and then literary management at the Goodman, St. Nicholas, and Milwaukee Repertory Theaters, and for the Midwest Playwrights Program and the Chicago Theater Project. Barbara continued to act and, initiating her true life's work, began to teach Shakespeare classes for Chicago actors.

How audacious! How dare she teach Shakespeare? What did she have to offer? She had her Northwestern degree and her Wallace Bacon pedigree, but certainly she wasn't recognized as a Shakespeare scholar or a deeply experienced Shakespearean actor or even as a director of record (whether of Shakespeare or anything else). Here was chutzpah! But ya know what? She was right. Because of teachers and mentors like Wallace Bacon, *something was going on* with Shakespeare in America, and Barbara was among the first-generation recipients of new thinking that proved to be wise thinking. I don't know whether she knew this empirically when she began teaching Shakespeare or merely understood it intuitively. Either way, because of Barbara and others of like mind across the country, there was a sea change in American classical theater of which even I became aware, but it took a few years, so allow me to backpedal.

Here's the deal: when Barbara and I were coming of age, every American actor approaching Shakespeare wanted to sound as British as he or she possibly could. It was the influence of the greats (already named above) who had The Voices and could follow a line of Shakespearean poetry forever and ever. Shakespeare seemed to sail, to take wing, on the music of the vocalization. The passion of the voice conveyed the emotion of the moment *even when the words didn't make sense to us*. NO one ever said to us, "Darling, you know you don't *have* to sound British," not even my British instructors in London.

After returning to the United States, I supported my evening theater work with a daytime job as an advertising copywriter ("America spells cheese K-R-A-F-T" is mine, I kid you not). I vacationed in London every year or eighteen months to take in theater: Peter Hall's *Hamlet* with Albert Finney at the National Theatre at the Old Vic, Peter Brook's Royal Shakespeare Company white-gymnasium *A Midsummer Night's Dream*, an astonishing *Edward II* at the National (still at the Old Vic). To this day, I'm the only American theater critic I know—and I ask my colleagues about this—who has seen six different productions of *Edward II*, among them one in the upstairs black box at Chicago Shakespeare Theater in 2008 (directed by Sean Graney).

And then there came a period of nine or ten years during which I didn't return to London at all. It was during this time that Barbara launched Shakespeare Repertory Theater, as it was called until it moved to Navy Pier, with her now-legendary $3,000 production of *Henry V* in the beer garden of the Red Lion Pub, on Lincoln Avenue just a block down from Orphans. Her Henry was young Si Osborne, very much in the blond-haired-blue-eyed tradition of the role, who had been one of Barbara's Shakespeare students, as were so many of the actors she has used repeatedly over the years. It wasn't just the charm and delight of the physical production that made it a hit, with battles happening between and in the beer garden trees, but the vigor and clarity of the acting. Barbara never looked back from this modest launching pad. When it comes to Shakespeare, it was Chicago's own beer hall putsch.

During this same period of years, I twice visited the Oregon Shakespeare Festival where some of my old Tufts friends—Peter Silbert, Megan Cole, William Hurt—were in the company. I was aware there, too, that there was a new clarity to the presentation of Shakespeare. At this time (and for many years afterward), I was a site reporter for the National Endowment for the Arts, visiting nonprofit theaters large and small across the country, and encountering Shakespeare (although not exclusively Shakespeare) good, bad, and indifferent. The best of it matched what I was seeing and hearing in Barbara's productions, and what I'd found at the Oregon Shakespeare Festival.

What I was seeing and hearing was *American* Shakespeare. Our actors coming of age in the 1970s and 1980s finally were moving beyond the compulsion to sound British. Once you discarded a put-on accent or dialect, and the line of the verse for its own sake, a new world opened up, and that was the world of Wallace Bacon: don't worry about the poetry. Make sense of the words *first* as expressions of character and intention, and the flow of the language will follow. And speak the speech, I pray you, as well-trained American actors (or Canadian actors, for that matter), not as well-trained American actors trying to sound British.

Every time I went to see a Chicago Shakespeare Theater show, I heard things—I *understood* things—that previously had passed me by in even the most familiar plays. Sometimes they were profound understandings, sometimes they were simple ideas or jokes or ironies of the moment. Every production, therefore, was refreshing, as if I were seeing and hearing the play for the first time. Dear God, I was a virgin again and again! And that sense of freshness remains today when I visit Navy Pier.

The upshot—or at least one upshot—is that when I finally returned to London, I rushed to the wonderful Cottesloe Theatre at the new Royal National Theatre complex to see Fiona Shaw in the title role of *Richard II*. The physical intimacy of the Cottesloe was wonderful, and every actor was first-rate . . . and it all sounded so absolutely phony to me! Every actor, it seemed to my ears and altered sensitivities, was playing the language and not the character, playing the words but not the sense. I understood that evening what Barbara Gaines had achieved back in my own home town, and how she and her work had helped me mature and grow as a theater lover, as an astute (presumably) member of the audience and as a theater critic, too. I continue to treasure every trip I make to the CST precincts at Navy Pier, never mind that it has the best damn views of the city skyline and lakescape in the whole damn city!

I remember so well, too, those words I had with Barbara back when we were seventeen and cherubic at Northwestern, sharing a Coke after rehearsing *A Month in the Country*. "But, Babs," I said, "what about Shakespeare?"

"Shakespeare?" she said. "Gosh, I've never thought about Shakespeare."

And so you see, I was the one. Nice to talk to you. Have a good day.

4

The Spatial Rhetoric of
Chicago Shakespeare Theater

JONATHAN WALKER

Chicago Shakespeare's Courtyard Theater combines the expansive scenic area of a deep-set, unframed proscenium stage with the intimacy
and versatility of a central, often bare, thrust stage, which reaches out to
touch the very heart of its auditorium. Occupying three vertical levels, the
Courtyard's auditorium embraces the thrust stage on three sides, arranging
as many playgoers to the stage's flanks as it does in front of the thrust. Such
a configuration between performance and spectatorial spaces is not entirely
novel among large-scale and high-budget theaters—the company's website,
for instance, states explicitly that its architects drew inspiration from the
Royal Shakespeare Company's Swan Theatre in Stratford-upon-Avon.[1] And
yet the hybrid nature of the Courtyard's design formulates spatial relationships between the action and the audience that are paralleled by very few
professional theaters. Of course not all of the theater's productions utilize
its proscenium and thrust spaces in the same ways, though the auditorium
space is always fixed. The specific relationships that the interior architecture fosters between performances and playgoers comprise what I will be
calling the Courtyard's spatial rhetoric, within which different productions
and directors make various scenic or dramatic statements. The playgoers'
proximity to and physical points of view onto the stage offer opportunities

for highlighting thematic and characterological tensions in the dramatic action by capitalizing on the space itself. Some productions in the Courtyard Theater, in other words, construct dramatic meaning for their audiences not only through the delivery of dialogue, the blocking of actors, stage and costume design, and so on but also through a calculated staging of space, which taps into a vocabulary of physical placement and juxtaposition to express both dramatic conflict and harmony, division and alliance, and detachment and intimacy among the characters who populate its stage.

A few of the Courtyard's productions that have actively deployed space in these ways are the inaugural *Antony and Cleopatra* (1999), *The Tempest* (2002), *Julius Caesar* (2002–2003), and *Romeo and Juliet* (2010). Before discussing specific scenes, however, I should like to detail certain technical features of this theater, which will help to illuminate the spatial context in which these plays have been performed. First of all, the thrust portion of the stage measures 20' wide x 27' 8" deep (553.4 sf), stopping just shy of the auditorium's midpoint. One of the features that distinguishes this open stage from many others is its contiguous proscenium stage, which measures 42' wide x 28' deep (1,176 sf); see Figure 10. Incidentally, this proscenium is mere inches smaller than the apron stage that the master carpenter Peter Street built for Philip Henslowe's Fortune Theater in 1600, which was to measure 43' wide x 27' 5" deep.[2] From the front edge of the Courtyard's thrust to the extreme upstage of its proscenium, where overhead doors open onto a backstage area, the stage's total depth stretches over 61', and, in several productions, the playing space was extended yet farther into the backstage for a depth of nearly 88'. Both segments of the stage regularly make use of traps, though the height of the thrust is only two feet above the main floor surrounding it. In addition to the great depth and appreciable width of the theater's solid playing area, productions often press the vertical space above the stage into the service of performance, using a single fly system over the proscenium stage and independent rigging (but no built-in line sets) over the thrust. Characters' ascents into the fly space can have vastly different effects, as we shall see, but they all naturally tend toward the spectacular as bodies mount or hover at the eye-level of gallery patrons and, on occasion, even swing out above the audience on the main floor.

Turning to the space of the auditorium, we find that both galleries are rather shallow and steep, with the topmost providing only a single row of seating, and the Dress Circle below it furnishing two rows. Although the Courtyard Theater offers vantage points with greater and lesser visibility, no member of the audience sits more than thirty-eight feet from the stage, while not a few sit within only a couple feet of it. Figure 10 shows

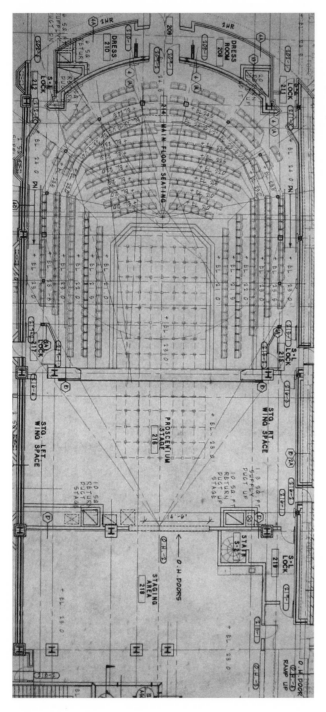

10. Architectural plans for the Courtyard Theater by VOA Associates Inc., version AR-7, sheet A2.06 (detail).

how seating on the main floor, like that in the galleries, follows the U-shaped perimeter of the auditorium, while also adding nearly two-fifths of the house's seats in the area forward of the thrust. The outer perimeter of the Courtyard's auditorium is particularly interesting with an eye to early modern theater history, insofar as the interior design emulates the same geometrical pattern by which amphitheaters like the Rose and the Globe were constructed in the late sixteenth century. As excavations and evaluations of the Rose and the Globe sites have shown, these two London amphitheaters—and probably most of the period's other open-air theaters—were built on polygonal designs, which oriented seated playgoers toward a central apron stage. Each of the polygon's bays that was devoted to spectatorial space contained raked seating and housed two galleries above a ground floor. In Figure 11, for example, a yard-level plan for the new Globe in London shows how the structure's polygonal shape distributes playgoers 270° around the stage, which, like the Courtyard's, extends to the center of the auditorium. By comparison, in Figure 12 we see that half of the Courtyard's auditorium is modeled on a sixteen-sided polygon, with seating governed by the centripetal orientation of each bay.[3]

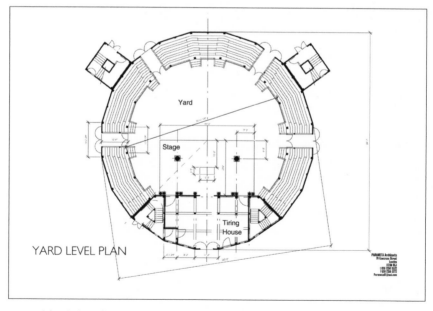

11. Yard-level plan of Shakespeare's Globe, London. Courtesy of Jon Greenfield, Globe Architect

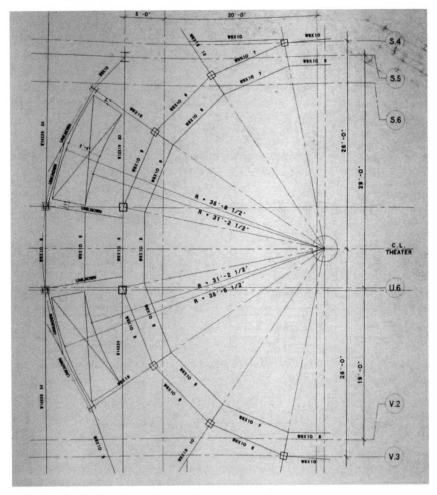

12. Architectural plans for the Courtyard Theater by VOA Associates Inc., version AR-10, sheet A4.03 (detail).

As suggested above, Courtyard spectators occupy positions both parallel and perpendicular to the thrust stage, which radically dehomogenizes the playgoing experience; see Figure 13. Theaters that utilize thrust, apron, transverse, and other open stages seek "to bring auditorium and acting area into the same architectural space and to get as close as possible a relation between the action of the play and the spectators watching it. The focus of the audience's attention is on the centre of the drama and members of that audience tend to group themselves round this focus."[4] In such theaters, this

61

"close ... relation between the action of the play and the spectators watching it" usually makes the dramatic tensions and conflicts represented in performance more physically immediate, and thus more powerful, to the audience. The Courtyard attains such immediacy partly by staging hundreds of its entrances and exits through the auditorium, which does not privilege any one spectatorial angle or viewpoint but instead multiplies the directionality of the performance up to at least 180° around the thrust stage. In contrast, traditional proscenium-arch theaters tend to compress their audiences' sightlines into narrower corridors that idealize the angle at which spectators observe the performance, thereby exercising more control over how playgoers perceive dramatic action. On the other hand, early modern amphitheaters offered spectators a degree of encirclement around the stage and, concomitantly, a freedom of perspective as well as physical mobility vastly greater than those of the Courtyard's. It is by mixing various components of these two designs that Chicago Shakespeare Theater achieves certain rhetorical effects through its staging of space.[5]

If the configuration between performance and spectatorial spaces in the Courtyard is fixed but also visually heterogeneous, giving playgoers a consistently broad array of physical positions and sightlines onto the dramatic action, then the primary way that the theater produces new spatial formations is through its manipulation of perspective on the thrust and proscenium stages. Although productions like Peter Brook's adaptation *The Tragedy of Hamlet* (2001) have been staged almost entirely on the thrust and others have dominated the proscenium, the size and the perpendicular arrangement of the two distinct but contiguous spaces enable directors to block characters and locate dramatic action either in very close quarters near the audience or at considerable distances upstage.[6] The manipulation of space is of course what all good directors do, and even the simplest stages of whatever size can craft a sense of both nearness and distance during performance. Yet, without being integrated into the thematic and characterological tensions of a dramatic fiction (those social conflicts and interpersonal strains around which the dramatic agon turns), physical nearness and distance on the stage are simply relative qualities with neutral values. Proximity does not really signify on its own. But when a production deploys space and physical juxtapositions in ways that both emphasize and interpret these dramatic tensions, then the space itself acquires significant meaning for playgoers.

For example, in representations of either demure or intense emotional intimacy, such as those involving lovers like Romeo and Juliet or Antony and Cleopatra, the downstaging of action tends to reproduce those feelings of intimacy—sometimes coupled with voyeurism—within individual audi-

13. Chicago Shakespeare's Courtyard Theater. Photograph by Steinkamp-Ballogg Photography, Chicago

ence members, who observe characters touching, kissing, and embracing while they themselves sit very near to these gestures of closeness. On the other hand, if *Richard II*'s Northumberland, Willoughby, and Ross gather at the edge of the stage to lament Henry Bolingbroke's exile and to insist that "The King's grown bankrupt like a broken man,"[7] then their physical proximity to the audience activates a different kind of intimacy, one involving treasonous secrets and plots that transform the downstage space they occupy into a site of anxious or cloying conspiracy. The strategic upstaging of scenes often produces similar correlations between playing space and dramatic action. At the conclusion of *Richard III*, for instance, the new King Henry VII declares victory over the dead king and prays to his God:

> Enrich the time to come with smooth-faced peace,
> With smiling plenty, and fair prosperous days.
> Abate the edge of traitors, gracious Lord,
> That would reduce these bloody days again
> And make poor England weep forth streams of blood.[8]

Just prior to this speech in the Courtyard's 2009 production, the eleven ghosts who had earlier blessed Henry and cursed Richard were standing in a line across the upstage area, invoking a visual impression of the devastation caused by the Wars of the Roses. Yet, after the new king speaks the play's concluding lines and exits, the ghosts back up in succession and recede into the darkness, suggesting that under Henry's rule this devastation would now be moving into the past instead of haunting the present.[9] Conversely, Julius Caesar's triumphal entry at the opening of the 2002–2003 production began inside a small corridor that issued from the backstage area onto the proscenium. As the emperor's entourage filed out of the passageway, which was initially lit only from within, it engulfed the stage and proceeded onto the thrust, where light likewise flooded the scene. Reminiscent of entering a coliseum, the procession communicated an image of grandeur through the vast distance it covered and the throngs of followers celebrating Caesar's rule.[10]

The contrast produced by upstage and downstage character-groupings is also a potent means for exposing divisions and proclaiming alliances within the social fabric of a play, especially in a space like the Courtyard's. In the same production of *Julius Caesar*, Cassius and the other conspirators visited Brutus at home early in act 2. The thrust was lit dimly with blue light, signifying nighttime, and the proscenium was largely in darkness. After Brutus's servant Lucius announced their unexpected visit, saying "half their faces [are] buried in their cloaks, / That by no means I may discover them / By any mark of favour,"[11] the conspirators entered slowly through the same upstage passageway that Caesar had used in the opening scene, and they then assembled into two single-file lines, suggesting their tight militaristic discipline. Meanwhile, Brutus moved down and sat on the steps at the corner of stage left, meditating on the threat of conspiracy while glancing back toward the entering group. He said:

> They are the faction. O conspiracy,
> Sham'st thou to show thy dang'rous brow by night,
> When evils are most free? O then by day
> Where wilt thou find a cavern dark enough
> To mask thy monstrous visage? Seek none, conspiracy. (2.1.77–81)[12]

From any seat in the auditorium, Brutus appeared separate, even isolated, from the men on the proscenium, creating a great spatial gulf that bespoke his distance from the others' political positions. That the conspirators were visible but shrouded in darkness corresponded vividly with Brutus's lines above, but the fact that he was himself in near-darkness and in a marginal

location during this scene suggested that he may not be as politically re-
mote as his words and physical distance from the others implied. Eventually,
they would all mingle and bathe their hands together in the blue light of
the thrust. By spatializing and lighting them in these ways, the production
staged the initial political divide between these characters. But it also staged
Brutus's humanity and his own self-division, making it difficult for playgoers simply to vilify him.[13]

The 2001 production of *Richard II* used a similar spatializing technique
to differentiate political positions, though instead of manipulating the horizontal planes of foreground and background as *Julius Caesar* would do the
following year, the confrontation scene between Richard and Bolingbroke at
Flint Castle employed a visual vocabulary of physical height and lowliness.[14]
The earliest printed text of *Richard II*, a 1597 quarto, offers the stage direction: "*Richard appeareth on the Walls*,"[15] which is to say that he enters with his
men in an elevated position, probably in a gallery above the stage (originally
at The Theater in Shoreditch), while Bolingbroke and his men remain below
on the stage. After Bolingbroke learned that Flint Castle lodged the king, in
the Courtyard production he and his men began to exit through the auditorium, when suddenly Richard appeared brightly lit on a very high platform
in the space above where the proscenium and thrust meet. He stood tall, he
was crowned, he wore regal accoutrements, and he was surrounded by his
loyal advisors, as light beamed down from above as if bestowing a divine
blessing. Moreover, Richard was commanding and emphatic in his speeches
to Bolingbroke's envoy Northumberland, controlling the scene both aurally
and visually. When Northumberland returned to the darkened aisle of the
auditorium to confer with Bolingbroke, however, Richard weakened and
collapsed to his knees, saying to Aumerle: "We do debase ourself, cousin, do
we not, / To look so poorly and to speak so fair?" (3.3.126–27), which put
the visual splendor that playgoers had just witnessed into tension with Richard's own degraded self-perception. To be sure, the king had already given
up before the fight—had given up to avoid the fight—so when Northumberland returned and said of Bolingbroke, "My lord, in the base court he doth
attend / To speak with you. May it please you to come down?" (3.3.175–76),
Richard replied, "In the base court: base court where kings grow base / To
come at traitors' calls, and do them grace" (3.3.179–80).[16]

The differential between the king's height and his subjects' lower status
is a conventional social figure that also expresses their political relationship. The text activates this figure through its language—"debase," "poorly,"
"base court," "come down," and so forth—and, as already suggested, the 1597
quarto's stage direction for Richard's entry aloft makes the sociopolitical

relationship between the king and his subjects more intelligible and poignant. The production's physical elevation of Richard above other characters and audience members alike is an obvious enough image of the king's superior standing, but the positioning of Bolingbroke and his allies in an aisle of the auditorium introduces fascinating convulsions both to the audience's subordinate relationship with Richard and to its lateral relationship with Bolingbroke. If we are all subject to Richard's visual and rhetorical dominance in this scene, then Bolingbroke's invasion and occupation of spectatorial space reenacts his invasion and occupation of English soil, from which the king had earlier banished him for six years. In both the dramatic fiction and in the theater, in other words, Bolingbroke audaciously strides through places where he doesn't belong. And since he so readily shares the audience's territory in this and other scenes, Bolingbroke literally associates himself and his sedition with playgoers, who certainly hold different attitudes and degrees of sympathy toward him as well as toward the king, but who are also obliged to tolerate his occupation of their space—a political predicament not unlike Richard's own. By taking advantage of the Courtyard's substantial fly space as well as the permeable barrier between the thrust and the auditorium, the staging of this scene drew spectators' own physical positions into the meaning of the play, making them participants in, and not just passive observers of, Richard II's downfall.

Whatever playgoers might think about the legitimacy or the corruption of Richard's reign, on the one hand, or about the treason or the justification of Bolingbroke's deposition of the king, on the other, the Courtyard's staging of this scene demonstrated how the very notions of majesty and authority are both constructed and efficacious. That is, although majesty and authority were here fashioned out of spectacular symbolic materials such as Richard's crown and regalia, his visually dominant position, and his imposing voice, they also exercised real power through their awe-inspiring display, in spite of their constructedness. Playgoers were made to feel this power during his long, commanding speech to Northumberland denouncing Bolingbroke's impudence, which is why the evacuation of that power was so startling a sight when he fell to his knees on the elevated platform. The 2002 production of *The Tempest* likewise inspired a sense of great power through dazzling and lofty spectacle, but when the scene's artifice revealed itself to the audience it did not diminish Prospero's authority, as Richard's collapse diminished his, but enhanced it. Act 4, scene 1 opened on the thrust stage with Prospero lecturing Ferdinand about the "rich gift" of his daughter Miranda, whose "virgin-knot" he must not untie "before / All sanctimonious ceremonies may / With full and holy rite be ministered."[17] The two lovers sat together on a large swing as Prospero spoke. He then set the swing in motion, and it rose into the air, mounting above the audience seated in front of the stage on the main floor.

Thus began the play's masque scene, wherein the goddesses Iris, Juno, and Ceres sang a marriage blessing to the lovers. Clad in long white dresses and masks, the three figures seemed to float sideways onto the proscenium from the wings as the stage lighting shifted to a numinous dark blue and as Prospero took a seat on the edge of the stage. Halfway through their serenade, Iris, Juno, and Ceres began to ascend together, creating a visual harmony to match their melodic one. Even as they rose to the very top of the proscenium opening, the thick gatherings in their skirts continued to unfurl, extending many yards to the stage below. The goddesses hovered there singing, when Prospero abruptly roused himself and said:

> I had forgot that foul conspiracy
> Of the beast Caliban and his confederates
> Against my life. The minute of their plot
> Is almost come. (4.1.139–42)

The urgency of this matter demanded that Prospero end the masque and call on Ariel for assistance, and so he said to the goddesses, "Well done! Avoid; no more!" (4.1.142).[18] At this point in the action, the first printed text of *The Tempest* in the 1623 folio supplies the stage direction: "*Prospero starts sodainly and speakes, after which to a / strange hollow and confused noyse, they heauily vanish.*"[19] What "*a / strange hollow and confused noyse*" sounded like in the early modern theater is difficult to say, but when Prospero shouted: "Well done! Avoid; no more!" in the Courtyard's production, bright light immediately flooded the scene, exposing a rather stagey set in the background as the floating goddesses ungracefully drifted back to the wings. Further, playgoers could distinctly hear mechanical sounds from the fly-rigging as it wheeled the three figures out of sight, which was accompanied by the kind of jarring motions one would expect from suspended bodies being trailed by wires: "*they heauily vanish.*"

At one moment Prospero orchestrates a spectacular vision in the airspace over the proscenium stage, and in the next he dispossesses it of its brilliance. While the *Richard II* and *The Tempest* productions each put magnificent power on display and then suddenly exposed their theatrical artifice, there was an important difference between them. The supremacy that Richard projected from his elevated position at first appeared as natural as can be, which is but one mythology of kingship, yet his collapse undercut that appearance precisely because it was involuntary and therefore beyond his sovereign control. The high platform that would seem merely to be a symbol of Richard's innate majesty he revealed, in fact, to be its prop. On the other hand, Prospero never lost control over his masque as he commenced and concluded it at will. That he could ostensibly call on, conduct, and dismiss three goddesses as he pleased only reinforced his power; and, in exercising it, he did not need to exalt himself to a superior position, since he remained just as potent from below. In his review of the Courtyard production, David G. Brailow wrote of this scene:

> Prospero breaks off the masque with disproportionate rage, modulating into bitter sadness through the speech on the insubstantiality of life. [Larry] Yando makes it clear that, while Caliban is no real threat, the thought of Prospero's failure to control and civilize him fills him with a deep sense of futility and loss. The limits of his power remind him of the limits of mortality itself.[20]

Both the *Richard II* and *The Tempest* productions, then, drew on a spatial rhetoric in which the physical elevation of characters—along with the trappings of royalty on one side and the aura of the supernatural on the other—persuaded spectators that they were witnessing exhibitions of great power. The calculated use of the theater's substantial vertical space in these scenes affected far more than the staging of pure spectacle, however. The spectacle first convinced playgoers of the power it represents, making that power real, but the revelation of its artifice showed playgoers both the efficacy and the credibility of spectacle, making the power of theater the more real.

While such contrasts between high and low make the theater space signify in conjunction with political distinctions already embedded in the dramatic action, the oppositional staging of characters and sets evokes other kinds of social configurations and conflicts. The Courtyard's 2010 production of *Romeo and Juliet*, for example, featured building façades gazing at one another from opposite sides of the proscenium, with the playing space in between functioning as a street; in some scenes, the middle ground represented indoor space with the façades resembling an Italian villa's interior walls.[21] The buildings were necessarily angled upstage to increase playgoers' visibility, but this angling also had the advantageous effect of causing the set to recede from view, creating an implied vanishing point in the distance; see Figure 14. As with the deep entry corridor used in *Julius Caesar* (along with similar uses in other productions like *Antony and Cleopatra* [1999] and *The Merchant of Venice* [2005]), *Romeo and Juliet* extended its playing space into the backstage area beyond the overhead doors, which enhanced this

14. The set for Chicago Shakespeare Theater's 2010 production of *Romeo and Juliet*. Directed by Gale Edwards with scenic design by Brian Sidney Bembridge. Photograph by Liz Lauren

implied vanishing point during performance. Contributing to the sense of recession in space were three slightly trapezoidal grates built into the central floor of the proscenium, with another two on the thrust. Elongated and tapered toward the upstage, these metal grates allowed for indirect lighting from beneath as well as opportunities for trap use. Thus, the symmetrical positioning of the facades conveyed an impression of likeness as well as confrontation, which is precisely how the play's Prologue describes the Capulets and the Montagues:

> Two households, both alike in dignity
> In fair Verona, where we lay our scene,
> From ancient grudge break to new mutiny,
> Where civil blood makes civil hands unclean.[22]

When the action of the play began, A-frame construction barricades with flashing amber lights lined the middle of the street, sitting atop the central grates. Immediately, several metal garage doors in each of the façades flew open in unison, out of which stepped two groups of servants from the "two households." The swaggering and exchanging of insults between the Capulets and the Montagues inevitably resulted in a physical confrontation as the men threw and kicked down the barricades while attacking one another. The use of construction barricades, in particular, suggested that some Veronese authority had placed them there in the first place, but they did not provide any actual barrier, relying instead on law-abiding citizens to heed their silent warning. Dividing the households as they divided the street, the barricades were but a temporary and insubstantial solution to an already fragile peace, which the servingmen managed to destroy with ease. A complement to the street barricades, moreover, the scaffolding that covered much of the façade at stage right gave the appearance that the building was undergoing construction, which hinted that the household may also harbor disorder within its doors.[23] During the Capulets' masquerade ball a short while later, the audience observed just such disorder when Tybalt spied Romeo in the crowd and went "to strike him dead" (1.5.56). But the Capulet patriarch intervened, telling his nephew: "I would not for the wealth of all this town / Here in my house do him disparagement. / Therefore be patient, take no note of him" (1.5.66–68).[24] When Tybalt tried to disobey, Capulet threw him to the ground—the very ground, not coincidentally, where the opening brawl had occurred—and made his nephew submit. For the moment, Capulet had restored order to his household, but like the barricades it was precarious and subject to the volatility of youth.

The opening tableau's confrontation between two opposing building façades, which were in states of disrepair and were divided by construction barricades, offered playgoers a scenic metonym for the "ancient grudge" between "two households." Whenever the central playing area represented a street, then that space too acquired symbolic value in relation to the feuding families. Because the houses never managed to contain the conflict between the Capulets and the Montagues, the fighting routinely spilled out into the street, a common space where the inhabitants of Verona should be cultivating civil relationships instead of shedding "civil blood." The visual perspective created by the production's scenery, finally, and the implied vanishing point far upstage are familiar theatrical effects, which were popularized in the sixteenth century by Sebastiano Serlio, whose second book of *Tutte l'opere d'architettura* (1584) supplied early set designers with elaborate woodcuts for fashioning perspective scenery appropriate to comic, tragic, and satiric plays.[25] In the Courtyard's *Romeo and Juliet*, the visual perspective created by its receding set emphasized an uncertain but ominous conclusion to the play's action, since the vanishing point was obscured and the upstage was often cloaked in darkness. If streets are made for travel, then the destination toward which the dramatic fiction drives as it moves into the middle distance looks woeful indeed. For Romeo and Juliet, the street itself became "the fearful passage of their death-marked love," through which playgoers would likewise journey during "the two-hours' traffic of our stage" (Prologue 9, 12).

Chicago Shakespeare Theater's website showcases the configuration between performance and spectatorial spaces in the Courtyard, noting specifically the relationships that their arrangement fosters: "The design celebrates the importance of the audience in performance by surrounding the actors with the audience and the audience with fellow audience members. The intimacy of the 500-seat house serves to energize the work on the stage and the excitement in the seats."[26] Such physical intimacy can certainly help to make the playgoing experience less mediated by incorporating the audience into private, sometimes quite clandestine encounters between characters. But it can also alienate audience members—a valuable theatrical effect— by bringing conspiratorial, disconcerting, or even violent action a bit too close for comfort. Conversely, the depth of the proscenium gives the theater the flexibility to forgo the intimacy associated with the thrust in order to stage either more grandiose or more desolate scenes from a distance, which downstage space is less effective at conveying persuasively. The sizable fly space, too, can put great power on display through stunning spectacle, just as it can reveal emptied-out power consisting of little more than its faltering exhibition. With the capacity to position scenes either very near to or very far from the audience, both on, around, and high above the stage, and also in several of these locations at once, the theater is able to exploit a wide vocabulary of space. Productions in the Courtyard frequently draw on this vocabulary to make visual assertions about the social divisions and alliances that are fundamental to dramatic action.

The central aim of rhetoric is to persuade an audience either to adopt or abandon a particular intellectual position, one that is based on a speaker's argumentative discourse. If the theater positions playgoers in seats that orient them toward a stage, and furthermore, if the stage delivers to them a dramatic discourse that is itself a narrative of conflicting intellectual or characterological positions, then live performance is at core a rhetorical enterprise that convinces spectators not to adopt a specific perspective—at least not in worthwhile theater—but to observe and adjudicate between the multiple perspectives that its characters espouse. The size, shape, and design of the Courtyard's stage and auditorium maximize the potential for staging the physical space playgoers see, so that its nearness and distance, its height and lowness, and the juxtaposition between these locations might all signify in conjunction with the characters' relationships and the social conflicts that bring dramatic space into being.

NOTES

Acknowledgments: My thanks to Gina Buccola and Peter Kanelos for their invitation to contribute to this volume. I am also grateful to Jon Greenfield for the use of one of his drawings of the new Globe. At Chicago Shakespeare Theater, I would like to thank Susan Knill, Theater and Facility Manager, who gave me access to architectural documents and answered innumerable questions; to Marilyn J. Halperin, Director of Education and Communications, who is always as delightful as she is helpful; to Edward Leahy, Technical Director, who kindly provided me with essential technical information about the theater; to Elizabeth Neukirch, Public Relations Manager, for assistance acquiring several images; and to Ellen Shipitalo for furnishing me with crucial details about the *Richard III* production.

1. "Facility and Virtual Tour," Chicago Shakespeare Theater, accessed September 21, 2011.

2. The building contract for the Fortune Theater states that its "Stadge shall conteine in length ffortie and Three foote of lawfull assize and in breadth to extende to the middle of the yarde," which was to be fifty-five feet square. For a transcription of the contract, see R. A. Foakes and R. T. Rickert, eds., *Henslowe's Diary* (Cambridge: Cambridge UP, 1961), 308. The contract is housed at Dulwich College, Muniment 22.

3. For recent theater historical work on early modern playhouses and their archeology, see, for instance, Julian Bowsher and Pat Miller, *The Rose and the Globe—Playhouses of Shakespeare's Bankside, Southwark: Excavations 1988–91* (London: Museum of London Archaeology, 2009); and J. R. Mulryne and Margaret Shewring, eds., *Shakespeare's Globe Rebuilt* (Cambridge: Cambridge UP, 1997), especially John Orrell, "Designing the Globe: Reading the Documents," 51–65, and Jon Greenfield, "Design as Reconstruction: Reconstruction as Design," 81–96.

4. Roderick Ham, ed., *Theatre Planning* (Toronto: U of Toronto P, 1972), 17.

5. Although the Courtyard Theater's acoustical properties are beyond the scope of this essay, I will note that the space achieves a rich auditory environment through a mixture of both absorbent and highly reflective surfaces, including not only wood (mainly white ash) but also several rows of 45°-angled brick in the walls of the auditorium and air pockets built under the galleries, which effectively distribute sound without the booming reverberation associated with more rigid materials. For the acoustical properties of early modern theaters, see Bruce R. Smith, *The Acoustic World of Early Modern England: Attending to the O-Factor* (Chicago: U of Chicago P, 1999), especially chapter 8.

6. Adapted and directed by Peter Brook, *The Tragedy of Hamlet* ran from May 10 to June 2, 2001.

7. William Shakespeare, *Richard II*, in *The Norton Shakespeare: Based on the Oxford Edition*, ed. Stephen Greenblatt et al. (New York: W. W. Norton, 1997), 2.1.258.

8. William Shakespeare, *Richard III*, in *Norton Shakespeare*, 5.8.33–37.

9. Directed by Barbara Gaines, *Richard III* ran from September 23 to November 22, 2009. Gloucester/Richard III was played by Wallace Acton and Richmond/Henry VII by Brendan Marshall-Rashid.

10. Such staging decisions employ a parallel early modern practice wherein the performance aims to create a sense of immense crowding, usually indicated by permissive stage directions during mass entries like "*and others as many as can be*," a phrase that appears toward the opening of the first quarto of *The Most Lamentable Romaine Tragedie of Titus Andronicus* (London: Printed by Iohn Danter for Edward White and Thomas Millington, 1594), sig. A4ᵛ. See "permissive stage directions" in Alan C. Dessen and Leslie Thomson, *A Dictionary of Stage Directions in English Drama, 1580–1642* (Cambridge: Cambridge UP, 1999), 161–62. Running from December 7, 2002, to February 23, 2003, *Julius Caesar* was directed by Barbara Gaines.

11. William Shakespeare, *Julius Caesar*, in *Norton Shakespeare*, 2.1.74–76.

12. In the Courtyard production, Brutus was played by Kevin Gudahl, Cassius by Scott Parkinson, and Lucius by James McKay.

13. In his review of *Julius Caesar*, directed by Barbara Gaines, Chicago Shakespeare Theater, Justin Shaltz wrote that "Gaines contrasts Brutus's role in the murderous conspiracy with his acts of compassion: he kneels before Portia to attend to her self-inflicted thigh wound, welcomes the aged Ligarius into his home, and finally shows tenderness toward the servant Lucius." *Shakespeare Bulletin* 21.2 (2003): 37–38, at 37.

14. Barbara Gaines directed *Richard II*, which ran from September 7 to November 18, 2001.

15. *The Tragedie of King Richard the Second* (London: Printed by Valentine Simmes for Androw Wise, 1597), sig. F4ᵛ.

16. Richard II was played by Scott Parkinson, Bolingbroke by Scott Jaeck, Northumberland by Fredric Stone, and Aumerle by Reginald Nelson.

17. William Shakespeare, *The Tempest*, in *Norton Shakespeare*, 4.1.8, 4.1.15–17.

18. Directed by Barbara Gaines, *The Tempest* ran from March 29 to June 16, 2002. Prospero was played by Larry Yando, Miranda by Cassandra Bissell, Ferdinand by Timothy Edward Kane, Iris by McKinley Carter, Juno by Ariane Dolan, Ceres by Deborah Monson, and Caliban by Scott Jaeck.

19. William Shakespeare, *The Tempest*, in *Mr. William Shakespeares Comedies, Histories, & Tragedies* (London: by Isaac Iaggard and Ed. Blount, 1623), sig. B2ʳ.

20. David G. Brailow, review of *The Tempest*, directed by Barbara Gaines, Chicago Shakespeare Theater, *Shakespeare Bulletin* 20.2 (2002): 18–19, at 19.

21. Directed by Gale Edwards with set design by Brian Sidney Bembridge, *Romeo and Juliet* ran from September 15 to November 21, 2010.

22. William Shakespeare, *Romeo and Juliet*, in *Norton Shakespeare*, Prologue 1–4.

23. I am grateful to Gina Buccola for reminding me of the scaffolding and suggesting this reading.

24. Capulet was played by John Judd, Tybalt by Zach Appelman, and Romeo by Jeff Lillico.

25. Sebastiano Serlio, *Tutte l'opere d'architettura* (Venetia: Presso Francesco de' Franceschi, 1584), "Della scena comica," sigs. G1ᵛ–G2ʳ; "Della scena tragica," sigs. G2ʳ⁻ᵛ;

"Della scena satirica," sigs. G3^{r-v}. Books I and II were first printed in Paris in 1545, and an English translation appeared in London in 1611. For reproductions of the three Serlian scenes, see Stephen Orgel, "Shakespeare Imagines a Theater," *Poetics Today* 5 (1984): 549–61, at 550–52.

    26. "Virtual Tour."

BIBLIOGRAPHY

Bowsher, Julian, and Pat Miller. *The Rose and the Globe—Playhouses of Shakespeare's Bankside, Southwark: Excavations 1988–91*. London: Museum of London Archaeology, 2009.

Brailow, David G. Review of *The Tempest*, directed by Barbara Gaines. *Shakespeare Bulletin* 20.2 (2002): 18–19.

Chicago Shakespeare Theater. "Facility and Virtual Tour." Accessed September 21, 2011.

Dessen, Alan C., and Leslie Thomson. *A Dictionary of Stage Directions in English Drama, 1580–1642*. Cambridge: Cambridge UP, 1999.

Foakes, R. A., and R. T. Rickert, eds. *Henslowe's Diary*. Cambridge: Cambridge UP, 1961.

Ham, Roderick, ed. *Theatre Planning*. Toronto: U of Toronto P, 1972.

Mulryne, J. R., and Margaret Shewring, eds. *Shakespeare's Globe Rebuilt*. Cambridge: Cambridge UP, 1997.

Orgel, Stephen. "Shakespeare Imagines a Theater." *Poetics Today* 5 (1984): 549–61.

Serlio, Sebastiano. *Tutte l'opere d'architettura*. Venetia: Presso Francesco de' Franceschi, 1584.

Shakespeare, William. *The Most Lamentable Romaine Tragedie of Titus Andronicus*. London: Printed by Iohn Danter for Edward White and Thomas Millington, 1594.

———. *The Norton Shakespeare: Based on the Oxford Edition*. Ed. Stephen Greenblatt et al. New York: W. W. Norton, 1997.

———. *The Tempest*. In *Mr. William Shakespeares Comedies, Histories, & Tragedies*. London: Printed by Isaac Iaggard and Ed. Blount, 1623.

———. *The Tragedie of King Richard the Second*. London: Printed by Valentine Simmes for Androw Wise, 1597.

Shaltz, Justin. Review of *Julius Caesar*, directed by Barbara Gaines. *Shakespeare Bulletin* 21.2 (2003): 37–38.

Smith, Bruce R. *The Acoustic World of Early Modern England: Attending to the O-Factor*. Chicago: U of Chicago P, 1999.

PART II

This One's for the Girls

Millennial Ladies in Josie Rourke's Twelfth Night

ALICIA TOMASIAN

By 2007 Chicago's new millennium had hosted two highly praised all-male productions of *Twelfth Night*, both at Chicago Shakespeare Theater. Until Josie Rourke's 2009 mixed-sex cast, CST fans might have begun to assume that the play's cross-dressing heroine, Viola, only made sense played by a man. These nods to Elizabethan casting perhaps gave new meaning to the character's plaint, "Disguise, I see, thou art a wickedness / Wherein the pregnant enemy does much."[1] For a time, the play's gender bending provided a platform for agendas precluding a female Viola. By contrast, the theater's third *Twelfth Night* of the millennium promised a more feminist approach, even in the choice of Rourke as director. Her 2005 *Much Ado About Nothing* had switched a number of the play's male roles (including Dogberry's watch) to female characters in what theater critic Charles Spencer bemoaned as the young director "making a feminist point" about women's intuition.[2] If Rourke was hired to reinstate a feminist gaze through Viola and Olivia, she certainly delivered. For my community-college students, most of whom saw the production in conjunction with a Shakespeare course they were taking with me, she did more than that. Drawing on Shakespeare's 400-year-old gender bending, she incorporated fresh young heroines to address a new generation of young women—straight, gay, or bisexual—convincing them that Shakespeare's androgynous erotics were all about them: their generation, their city, their desires, and their theatrical pleasure. While the all-male productions had been hugely popular, Rourke's *Twelfth Night* exemplified CST's specific appeal to a new audience, one bolstered by sales targeted at college groups, such as my own students at Harper College. Transforming CST's thrust stage into a 7,000-gallon pool splashing onto those groups, Rourke's production literally connected with the audience through the water some saw as representing personal freedom.[3] She invited young viewers to identify powerfully with Shakespeare's characters, almost as millennial peers.

In so doing, Rourke went back to the drawing board in the play's celebration of youth and, arguably, female strength, but with enough of a modern twist in the form of athleticism, racial ambiguity, and girly sass to aim directly at a fresh generation of female theater novices. Further, she invited the entire audience to participate in their gaze, one that defines itself through personal freedoms and various female subjectivities. I hesitate to label Rourke's production as feminist; the term *feminism* itself is something many of my current students disavow, including those who consistently promote feminist agendas in class discussion, as a term invoking overly political and sometimes anti-male sentiment. Even when I read in class the O.E.D.'s comparatively sterile definition of feminism—"advocacy of the rights of women (based on the theory of equality of the sexes)"[4]—I usually get no more than half of a given class to claim the title of feminist. In this respect, my students actually most closely embody what Jenny Coleman identifies as third-wave feminism, dedicated to personal freedom and personal narratives. My students, like the third wave Coleman describes, typically reject earlier generations' feminism as too political, stymieing individuality, complexity, and diversity.[5] Coleman also references a number of critics who see women of the new millennium rejecting feminism as "anti-men, anti-feminine; anti-family; over-prescriptive; interfering in private lives."[6] I recognize these attitudes in my students, which may explain their pleasure in Rourke's distinctly feminine Viola. Third-wave feminism most closely captures how many first-generation college women see themselves: strong yet feminine, sexually ambiguous but pro-men, progressive but not aggressive. Thus, although they usually reject the label of feminist, I read Rourke's approach and their enthusiasm for it as third-wave feminist.

Rourke's third-wave gaze introduced the play to a broad audience, more diverse, young, and less culturally and educationally elite than a second-wave feminist or a distinctly male homoerotic gaze might. In fact, to many of my students attending the production with me, Rourke's joyful, watery romp felt mostly like a teen "chick flick" (perhaps one of the recent Shakespearean adaptations, such as *Ten Things I Hate about You* or *She's the Man*). In his review for *Shakespeare Bulletin*, Samuel Park agreed, arguing Michelle Beck as Viola "played up the character's tomboy-ish quality, giving Cesario a convincing teenage swagger."[7] For Park, an adolescent Viola relating to a more authoritative Olivia made these characters "more contemporary in psychology,"[8] because it emphasized Olivia's attraction to a younger man and Viola's fascination with an older woman's power. While I would argue that neither of these phenomena is unique to the twenty-first century, my students did identify with two exuberant, aggressive, but girly leading ladies. *New City* saw Rourke's vision as "actually quite traditional,"[9] and the *Tribune's* Chris Jones praised it as "a happily organic homage both to traditional Shakespearean comedy, pretty much as the old fellow wrote it for land-locked London, as well as to those warm-weather pleasures of the water,"[10] but my students felt that the production made a splash in more ways than one. Rourke seemed to be targeting a new generation of women who believe they can be both totally feminine and assertive.

CST'S GROUNDLINGS

I took a group of about fifteen students to Rourke's production of *Twelfth Night* in 2009. It should be noted that my group, as is often the case with college groups, sat directly to the side of the stage, alongside Rourke's pool. CST's Group Sales department has always made a point of placing us in the first rows on either side of the thrust stage, even though college groups pay just $30 a student. Jonathan Baude, Group Sales Coordinator, explained, "Those seats on the right and left sides, those are fun seats. If those are open, that's one of our favorite places to put groups."[11] According to Chicago Shakespeare Theater's website, the thrust stage "necessitates an intimate, immediate relationship between actors and their audience."[12] My students' comments about the production during and just after the trip asserted their feeling of connection to the performers. This was especially the case with the women in my group. One young woman, who had been on several CST trips before, asserted that she thought this one the "Best! Play! Ever!"[13] She insisted to her classmates who had not attended that the lead actresses spoke right to her. "They were looking at us and talking to us!" she exclaimed. Several other women agreed with her. I asked if the men felt the same direct address. None said they did, although they agreed with their female classmates that the production intensely engaged the audience. According to Baude, this effect was deliberate: "The performances are designed with our [thrust] stage in mind, so I think it is really cool to sit on one of the sides." He described such an experience as "immersive," providing a "slightly unconventional view," and explained that it often adds to the spectacle when the most intimate relationships between actors and audience involve college groups. "You'll see people gasping, hooting, and hollering," he said.[14] Baude estimated that college groups, often with fifty or sixty people, attend an average of three nights a week.[15] Thus, they can radically shape the audience experience.[16] While I cannot recall whether any of my students hooted or hollered, we certainly gasped as characters fell into the pool, splashing us. I occasionally hear our happy, newly minted theater enthusiasts boast of being close enough to feel the spit and to look the actors in the eye, but *Twelfth Night* took this feeling of identification to a whole new level.

In class discussion after the trip both men and women agreed that, despite the Elizabethan dress, the performance felt contemporary to them; they saw the characters as their peers. All of the attendees had read *Twelfth Night* before the show. We had discussed it in class, even performing scenes, and indeed most of these students had loved the text. In particular, they loved the homoerotic aspects of attraction between Olivia and Viola as well as Orsino and Viola. In discussion after attending the production, they all talked about how relatable Rourke's production was to them, and they raved to their classmates about the pool as well as Michelle Beck's Viola. In class, several students described Beck in great detail, commenting on how attractive, feminine, and funny she was. While they had all enjoyed Shakespeare's challenge to traditional gender roles when we read the play, most felt that the production made this element more real for them. In other words, they agreed with Charles Spencer that Rourke had a thoroughly modern (feminist) agenda. Of course, my students were not theater critics or Shakespeareans (although one is now in the process of becoming the latter, and two have just completed certification to teach high school English). What I found to be important in their comments was the relationship they developed with the stage, their belief that the production catered to them, CST's groundlings.

With class discussion in mind, I was curious to see what they would remember two years later when I interviewed them about their impressions. I wanted to know whether, after seeing other productions and after transferring to four-year universities, they still felt as they had two years ago. I also wanted to know if their impressions would be different beyond the context of class. Most students on the trip were in one particularly vocal and lively section of Introduction to Shakespeare. They had all bonded quickly, and in fact, on the night of the trip, dinner conversation lingered on issues of romantic relationships. Although both men and women were vocal in class, very vocal women outnumbered men. Thus, I also wondered if men would reflect on the performance differently once out of the group. Using my notes from class discussion, I developed interview questions. I was not surprised that many of them remembered our general class discussions about gender, but I was shocked that so many of my former students remembered intricate details, such as the wooden heart-shaped frame of the set, the bare feet of the actors, and specific moments, such as falls and leaps into the pool. More than that, I was amazed by how many told me that Rourke's production made them want to return to CST whenever possible, how this show made them feel like CST was their chosen indulgence, their place.

In interviews two years later, many female students still felt that Rourke's production and leading ladies aimed squarely at them. However, even separated from the group, most of the men I interviewed continued to speak highly of the production. (Only one man from Introduction to Shakespeare, who seemed to enjoy the show at the time, criticized it two years later.) One of the men who loved the show told me, "The women made more of an impression." They were, he thought, "gesturing to the audience," giving him "the idea that they're who we are supposed to be relating to." Another student, a woman in her late twenties, brought two friends with her. All three were recent immigrants to the United States from South America, still struggling to learn English. The student, in fact, called me simply "teacher." Her group arrived late, as they came right from work, sporting jeans and carrying large cups of pop. Although the student I knew was hardworking, smart, enthusiastic, and intellectual (she is majoring in engineering), I was worried that she and her friends might find Elizabethan English an insurmountable barrier. It had, in fact, been an obstacle in class. Instead, they all experienced Rourke's production as a celebration—their girls' night out—and worth every penny. In the lobby afterward, they raved about the show, going on and on about how much fun it was. Two years later, my student, who had never before attended a play in English, told me, "Going to the show was actually the best way to understand the book. For me, English is a second language, but the play made it understandable. It was great!" She also related to Viola: "I found it appealing that the main character was a girl. It was like Shakespeare's play, but there was something different, something a bit more, a twist." One of her friends also said she felt immersed in the production due to our seats. "I had never had an opportunity to attend a play like that before," she said. "I have only been to theaters where you sit in front of the stage. We were a little more incorporated, so I felt like a part of the play." She added, "I loved when one of the characters jumped in the pool!" Over the next two years, the student made an effort to participate in a number of trips to CST. She was clearly won over to Shakespearean theater.

According to my students, even the first image of the show, the set, cued them to expect a female perspective. One young woman remembered the excitement of walking in and seeing designer Lucy Osborne's heart-shaped frame, recalling that she instantly thought, "It was pretty. . . . I guess it could be seen as more feminine. I thought it was cute!" The first few minutes of the production provided another strikingly "girly" image. Rourke made quick use of the set's most surprising feature, the large pool, dropping Michelle Beck (Viola) from the ceiling with a shocking splash. After an alarming pause, Beck surfaced, gasping for air and pulling herself out of the pool in wet, thin clothes revealing her curvy, womanly body as well as her very feminine facial features. To my students, this image of Beck endured, even though Osborne's Elizabethan costuming provided some impressive cover. (As Osborne explained in an interview, "The sexual ambiguity of clothes at that time is . . . really interesting, which is so helpful when Viola dresses as Cesario."[17]) Most of my students, however, never forgot the youthful, pretty, voluptuous Viola of her first appearance. Most said the costuming never really hid Beck's true gender (an effect perhaps amplified by the fact that Viola looked up to a taller Olivia), but that seems not to have been a problem. To the young women I interviewed, Beck's body *mattered*; it felt preferable to the more boyish Viola (Imogen Stubbs) we had watched in clips from Trevor Nunn's film. Said one young woman in her interview, "I liked it. It would have been a more distant thing if she was a woman who looked like a man, because I don't relate to that. It made her a more romantic figure." Incidentally, Beck's body seemed to matter to the young men in our crowd as well. One man described her as "feminine" and "elegant." Another commented that he felt it would have been hard to hide Beck's curvy, attractive figure.

Both the women and the men who attended agreed, to some degree, with Jean E. Howard's view of Viola's "'feminine' subjectivity,"[18] and, for the most part, with Nancy Lindheim's reading of Viola: "She is always female for us, regardless of what she wears; constant asides and speeches remind us that her fears or desires are those conventionally ascribed to women and girls."[19] Did this kill the play's homoeroticism? The woman who saw Viola as a romantic heroine argued, "I think it is more believable if she [Viola] is pretty and more womanly. If she just looked like another man, then why wouldn't she [Olivia] just fall in love with another man?" Asked if she thought this Olivia was gay, the student answered, "bi-curious." She also thought this element of the production might seem scandalous to older generations. Her grandmother would have hated it, she told me, because her grandmother would be offended by the homoeroticism already present in Shakespeare's play but accentuated in Rourke's production. For this student, the disguise never really hid the truth of the play, Viola's womanhood. This same woman, however, asserted that she felt the women of the production were girly *and* physically assertive. She saw the female leads as "stronger than the men. Their posture was always straighter, more aggressive, more powerful." In fact, she said, she barely remembers the men. "I focused more on the women. I think the production did that." Said another woman of Viola, Olivia, and Maria, "They weren't so much masculine, but just leaders."

Karen Aldridge as Olivia and Michelle Beck as Viola also offered my students another point of bodily identification as African American or mixed race. Most of my students felt this made them more relatable to a younger and more diverse audience. In interviews, one woman, a returning student in her forties, identified herself as mixed race and said she related to light-skinned Beck. Being mixed, she mused, pushes people to "put you in a box." (This student said she is almost always assumed to be African American, even though she is a quarter white.) Regarding the racial diversity of the cast, she said, "I think it has got to be purposeful . . . more people can connect to the characters." This student had previously attended performances with racially diverse casts. While she always appreciated such choices, she had never before read it as purposeful the way she read a mixed-race Viola and Sebastian. She said she also felt that the seemingly "mixed" appearance of Viola and Sebastian might have been playing on ideas of "mixed" gender, or indefinite identity. Rourke's interpretation of *Twelfth Night*, she said, asked, "Who am I? What am I supposed to be? Who am I expected to be?" Also notable was African American Ora Jones as Maria, of whom the returning student asked, "Did she do a neck roll?" She seemed to be indicating that Maria not only *appeared* to be African American, but also that she gestured like a black woman. For most of my students, Rourke's diverse cast defied the trap Lisa M. Anderson describes as a well-meaning attempt at overcoming racism. For Anderson, despite the good intentions of mixed-race casts, the results often range from "merely distracting to quite discomforting."[20] Anderson describes some mixed-race casting as "colorblind casting,"[21] but my students did not perceive Rourke's choices as "blind," even though some of them had perceived previous casts in this light. To my students, the bodies of the actors, black, white, mixed, men and—most important—women, were not to be ignored. They were invitations to a new generation of Windy City Shakespeare fans willing to dive in. They were also tools used by Rourke and her cast to express a generational shift, a subtle new approach to the breaking of boundaries or the growing insignificance of them.

"THAT 'YOU KNOW WHAT I MEAN' LOOK"

Key to the youthful exuberance of the production was what the *Chicago Reader* called "a giddy cast,"[22] dressed as Elizabethans but moving as millennials. One young woman told me that she loved the traditional dress with the twist of bare feet, which she says she noticed right away. It looked, she said, "Shakespearean but a little different." Of course, the bare feet made splashing in the pool possible, but it also gave the characters a more contemporary look and freedom of movement, if only because we rarely see actors in doublets, bodices, and ruffs but without shoes. For this student, that connection between Shakespeare's material and her contemporary world (including Chicago) also came through in Lucy Osborne's waterside setting. "It looked inspired by Navy Pier," she said, and then continued, "It made you more aware that they are by the beach." For her, the production felt at once traditional but also current. (The watery location of the theater was particularly immediate to a few of my students, who had taken the water taxi to Navy Pier.)

For a young audience, it would seem, the key to that contemporary access was mostly the female bodies and the way those bodies moved, addressing the audience. Contemporary gestures and the dynamics they created invited the women in my class to relate to the women of the play, cued by the playful splashing of water. As the *New City* review observed, "water, after all, can reveal gender and desire. . . . Meanwhile, a good portion of the audience, especially the younger end, mostly likes getting splashed."[23] Indeed, my group got multiple splashings, much to their amusement. Some said they felt the water was a reminder of gender bending or sensuality. Tellingly, the young woman who loved the bare feet described Illyria as "by the beach," not the sea, perhaps evoking the same sense of freedom a generation of spring breakers would associate with a beach. In fact, we attended the production just after our break, as the show ran from March 29 to June 7. Whether or not Osborne was considering spring break, she said she wanted "to give a sense of being on a really beautiful, hot summer holiday. . . . It's a very comfortable, hot place to lounge around."[24]

Splashes, sprinkles, and dunks often punctuated moments of confused gender identity as well as erotic excitement. As Orsino observed of his new favorite, "Diana's lip / Is not more smooth and rubious; thy small pipe / as the maiden's organ, shrill and sound, / And all is semblative a woman's part" (1.4.31–34), he sprinkled her with water.[25] Later, as the two listened to music, Orsino grabbed Cesario and threatened to throw her in as she struggled to free herself. Tellingly, Cesario did not jump in until the final scene, when

15. Michelle Beck (center) with cast of *Twelfth Night* (2009), directed by Josie Rourke. Photo by Liz Lauren

she revealed her identity to Sebastian. Both then plunged in at the same time, leaping from either side of the stage and meeting in the middle. Thinking of this moment, the returning student explained that she thought the pool equaled truth. "Water seems to add an element of freedom and clarity," she said. Of Viola's exuberant leap into the water, she gushed, "The joy she felt, you could feel it. She could release the masquerade and rinse off all that stuff." The pool also provided the opportunity to show Orsino in a relative state of undress, without his ruff. Osborne clearly seized on Elizabethan attitudes regarding dress, opting to have Orsino at times forgo a ruff, which, by the time of the original performance of the play, was an androgynous accessory. Meanwhile, both Olivia and Viola (as well as Cesario) wore one. "It's an age where the men are trying to emulate Elizabeth I and become more feminine, and the women, also because of Elizabeth I, are becoming masculine," Osborne observed.[26] Contemporary audiences most often associate a ruff with Elizabeth, so it would make sense that this gender-neutral accessory would be an important part of costuming in this production. Yet Orsino's many dips into the pool allowed for a bare chest and neck, revealing an obviously masculine physical trait (chest hair).

Indeed, Orsino's more casual bare neck contrasted with Olivia's ruff in the promotional poster, although in her first appearance as Olivia, Aldridge clearly expressed sassy, girly, uncontained excitement over Cesario. As she became increasingly interested in her disguised visitor, she looked out to spectators audibly responding to her. After Cesario left, she rehashed their conversation—"What is your parentage?" (1.4.284), she repeated, then pounded her fists against her skirt and groaned in embarrassment. Calming herself, she continued, "'Above my fortunes, yet my state is well; I am a gentleman,' I'll be sworn thou art! / Thy tongue, thy face, thy limbs, actions and spirit do give thee fivefold blazon" (1.5.285–88). She punctuated this thought with a loud "woooo!" of passionate sexual attraction. Then, seemingly having worked herself into a frenzy, she slapped her chest a few times, as if catching her breath while she exclaimed, "Not too fast! Soft, soft" (1.5.288). (One of my students remembered this moment as Olivia fanning herself because Cesario was so "hot.") This received a big laugh, clearly inspired by her "giddy" excitement. Still breathless, she threw her arms in the air and yelled, "Well, let it be" (1.5.293). The more excited she got, the more contemporary seemed her side utterances and gestures. The returning student remembered a moment when "she came right to the edge of the stage and gave that 'You know what I mean' look right at the audience." Another of the women described her behavior as "like a high school girl," adding, "The gestures . . . were all more modern, but they really did seem timeless." One of the men, asked about Olivia, exclaimed, "I thought she was great! She seemed modern." (Her youthful demeanor also seemed in stark contrast to Mark L. Montgomery's slightly balding Orsino.) Aldridge's Olivia seemed to bounce and bound about in erotic excitement; her essence was far more girlfriend than countess. As she ordered Malvolio, "hie thee," she actually galloped to send the message home. Forfeiting all control, she called out, "I do I know not what, and fear to find / Mine eye too great a flatterer for my mind. / Fate, show thy force" (1.5.303–5). With that, she fell backward in joyful abandon, skirt, ruff, veil, and all, into the pool. As she willingly threw herself into the deep end, the audience applauded, wiping themselves dry. Aldridge's Olivia washed away all facade, literally and figuratively, in a gesture of youthful exuberance. While it was surprising to see her voluminous clothes immersed, her hair and makeup were clearly natural enough that she looked herself as she emerged, dripping.

Telling us, "You know what I mean," with her "look," she demanded of us to share her gaze. Her third-wave feminism invited even my self-identified straight female students to feel and understand Olivia's attraction to pretty, womanly Cesario/Viola. When the two women met for a second time, Olivia began the scene with composure but finally could not contain herself. Hilariously trotting up to Cesario as she waved her hands, she fawned, "Cesaaaarioooo," then confessing, "by the roses of the spring, / By maidenhood, honor, truth, and everything, I love thee so that, maugre all thy pride, / Nor wit nor reason can my passion hide" (3.2. 148–52). Clearly, many of my students felt complicit in this adolescent adoration, and many enjoyed the homoerotic tension. There were several moments during Olivia and Cesario's first meeting when Olivia nearly kissed Cesario, and during their second encounter, Olivia grabbed a squirming Cesario around the chest from behind, palming her disguised breasts. Aldridge's confused look won increasing laughter as she then fondled her own breasts for a point of comparison.

All of my students noted the sexual tension between women. Many also felt that Sebastian's more feminine features invited a certain pleasurable androgyny. I asked the woman in her forties about the appeal of a more feminine Cesario and Sebastian that we had discussed in class two years before. She thought for a moment, then began with the disclaimer, "I'm not gay." Contemplating Sebastian, who she thought "looked a little feminine," and Viola, she confessed, "I was attracted to him [Sebastian], but I couldn't help but be attracted to her too!" Struggling to describe her response to Beck, she said, "I'm trying to think of another word for 'masculine.' She didn't act butch. She was assertive without being aggressive." Tellingly, this student rejected traditional terms for her gaze and attraction, much the way third-wave feminists challenge traditional sex- and gender-based identifications. While her response to androgyny was no doubt largely the result of Shakespeare's original play, her reaction also clearly resulted from her twenty-first-century understanding of female sexuality as well as her response to Beck's person and performance. Finally, this student came to the conclusion that Beck's feminine beauty and presence as well as masculine disguise sparked her erotic gaze. "When she first came out [of the water] and she was so stunning, my admiration for the beauty was there," she recalled. "Then I was attracted to an assertive, attractive, intelligent woman." Animated, she continued, "I remember Viola came right to the corner of the stage and looked right at me, right through me. She was talking about how she felt as a woman, but looking at her as a man was sexually confusing because she was so cute!" This student experienced her interpretation as enjoyment of both hetero- and homoeroticism, but all within the context of appreciating traits she saw as feminine. The traditionally aged college women had similar responses; besides the woman who identified Olivia as "bi-curious," another, who attended with her fiancé, complained that Sebastian was "not feminine enough!" Initially, it seemed Olivia agreed. Perhaps because of Sebastian's submission to the lady's request, "Would thou'dst be ruled by me!" (4.2.63), the male version seemed unable to arouse Olivia's erotic excitement as had Cesario. The couple began walking off stage, arm in arm, quiet and composed, until Olivia turned back to face the audience (her girlfriend confidantes) and released a loud squeal of infatuation and triumph.

It was Beck's Viola, however, who obviously cultivated the closest relationship with young female patrons, using eye contact and body language to assert a strong female physicality. As she came to the awkward realization of Olivia's devotion—"She loves me, sure!" (2.3.22)—she looked squarely out at the first rows. To Orsino's misogynist observations, "Women are as roses, whose fair flower / Being once displayed, doth fall that very hour" (2.4.38–39), she once again looked out at the audience, reminding them of the woman beneath the doublet. She then responded wistfully, "Alas that they are so" (2.4.40). While none of the men I spoke to commented on these moments, all of the women did. Said one, "It definitely felt like the women were looking at the audience more than the men. . . . There were at least three different times when Viola and Olivia made eye contact with *me*." These moments were often accompanied by modern gestures of familiarity and sarcasm. Some of the most obvious sarcasm involved interactions with Orsino. Draping his arm around Cesario, the duke invited her to sit by the pool and listen to Feste's odd love song, which in class many of my students identified as "emo" (emotional). As explained to me in class discussion before the trip, "emo" most often refers specifically to music but also some-times to those who listen to emo music, as in the term "emo boy." This term also implies effeminacy. According to Urbandictionary.com, "the emo boy is a xy [*sic*] chromosome-based apology for the sinful excess of patriarchal society, achieved chiefly through the adoption of more stereotypically femi-nine traits," and as a group, emo boys "gather much of their inspiration from the more nihilistic aspects of 1980s rock/punk bands, typically due to it's [*sic*] prolifically morose tones and androgynous fashion."[27] Orsino's choice of song, then, helps to define him as an "emo boy," and in this production, so did Orsino's response to the music. As Feste sang, "Come away, come away death, / And in sad cypress let me be laid. / Fly away, fly away breath; / I am slain by a fair cruel maid" (2.4.51–54), the duke nodded to the music, then he covered his face in dramatic, exaggerated emotion. Viola watched his reaction and rolled her eyes. (One of the men in our group specifically recalled this gesture two years later.) Beck then looked away, seemingly sti-fling a chuckle. As the morbid love anthem continued, "My shroud of white, stuck all with yew; / Oh prepare it! / My part of death, no one so true / did share it" (2.4.51–56), Orsino threw himself onto his back, freeing Viola, who used the moment to stretch her arms. Looking back at his pathetic display, she shook her head. No longer able to lie still, "emo" Orsino got up to pace as Feste sang, "Not a friend, not a friend greet / My poor corpse, where my bones shall be thrown" (2.4.61–63). At this point, Viola turned away again, fighting to contain her laughter.

My students had been looking forward to this scene, and they were not disappointed. Beck's mocking gestures made a big impression on them. A few said how surprised they were and how much they enjoyed it that she seemed to be making fun of Orsino's lovesickness. "The men were more ridiculous than the women, because they just seemed like they didn't know what to do with themselves," one woman said. "You could totally see there was a power shift." In Jean Howard's reading, the play celebrates "a cross-dressed woman who does not aspire to the positions of power assigned to men,"[28] but Rourke took this idea and turned it upside down. For Howard, Viola's heterosexual desires render her unthreatening, but in Rourke's new vision, Viola's heterosexual desire underscored the ridiculousness of men, particularly Orsino.[29] While it is true that my students never forgot Viola's heterosexual desires, as Howard suggests, a millennial Viola used her dis-guise to mock and critique the very man to whom she was attracted. In response to Feste's jest, "The Lady Olivia has no folly. She'll keep no fool, sir, till she be married" (3.2.33), Viola laughed and nodded, clearly thinking of Orsino. That being said, one of the men told me, "It was not the mockery of men I expected it to be. They made it more fun." He clearly felt complicit in playful female subjectivity.

On a number of other occasions, Beck adopted certain gestures and movements that the world of the play presented as masculine, but contemporary young women saw as just confident and sporty. In her first appearance as a boy, she slapped the backs and arms of Orsino's men as they came out of the pool. Later, intermission concluded with a few musicians performing as Cesario watched and danced a bit in the form of some stiff knee bends, applauding with us as the piece ended and the house lights came down. Bantering with Feste, she joked about how she was "almost sick" for a beard, assuring the audience "though I would not have it grow on my chin" (3.1.46–47). Then, in response to a few laughs from the first rows, Beck pointed to the spectators, seemingly crediting them for getting the joke. This in turn won a big laugh from the crowd, during which she continued to stare down the front row, tsk-tsking them with her fingers. She seemed to be implying that we might be having too much fun at her expense or risking exposing her identity. Still, it was clear we were laughing with her, not at her. She was also complicit in the bawdry of the play, obviously pulling at the crotch of her pantaloons as she punned, "A little thing / would make me tell them how much I lack of a man" (3.4.302–3). Preparing to fight, her small, feminine frame seemed athletic, even as she flexed her muscles and gave herself a little slap to bring herself to attention. Like Aldridge, she used her bare feet to spring about the stage in movement neither graceful nor quite androgynous, but nimble, silly, and powerfully communicative: a new kind of woman. She obviously did not want to fight. (In fact, she briefly fainted at the thought, coming to with a slap on the arm from Fabian, which she returned. The two then exchanged two more slaps, with hers hard enough to push him.) Yet she was agile enough that she probably wouldn't have been half bad. Warming up, she shook out her hands and ran in place like a boxer. She took a few practice swings, one of which was forceful enough that Fabian jumped back in alarm.

While her heterosexual desire may, as Howard suggests, naturalize her in a potentially unstable world,[30] her final affirmation of that desire in the production rewrote traditional rules of women in courtship. In the text, Orsino initiates physical contact, asking Viola, "Give me thy hand, / And let me see thee in thy woman's weeds" (5.1.272–73), but in Rourke's production, Viola initiated true physical intimacy. Montgomery's Orsino kept an obvious, uncomfortable distance, holding his arm between himself and Beck as he delivered the lines, "Cesario, come— / For so you shall be, while you are a man; / But when in other habits you are seen, / Orsino's mistress, and his fancy's queen" (5.1.385–88). This moment seemed like an overt attempt to kill any male homoeroticism. He turned to walk away, while Beck looked out at the audience, as if for confirmation or guidance, then looked back at him. Suddenly, she grabbed him and pulled his face down to hers for a passionate kiss. In a complete reversal of stereotypically gendered seductions, he resisted briefly before wrapping his arms around her in a tight embrace.

"NOT THE HELPLESS FEMALE"

The final effect of Josie Rourke's third-wave feminism was one of empowerment, access, and freedom. The youthful, exuberant gesturing of the women no doubt assisted viewers unfamiliar with the play, unfamiliar with theater, and unfamiliar even with English. My community-college students are working hard to afford and excel in college, trying to lift themselves out of difficult economic situations. Rourke's production reminded them of themselves. They saw in both Viola and Olivia a self-determination, a powerful struggle to better one's circumstances. They also saw no threat in these traits. Rather, it seemed, most believed that such ambition made women more attractive to millennial men, both on stage and off. While all the women I spoke to said they felt the show was aimed primarily at women, they all said they would recommend it to male friends. Tellingly, nearly all the men I spoke to really enjoyed it, also saying they would recommend it to male friends, although one specified that he would recommend it only to his more sensitive male friends. Perhaps they related to Orsino, who was essentially rescued from his folly by Viola.

Just as Viola's heterosexual desire became an opportunity to take control of Orsino, her distress, as experienced by my students, became an opportunity for her to show strength. One of the young women wistfully remarked, "Seeing her in distress, drowning in the first scene—you actually see her all wet—it made her seem like more of a romantic heroine." But then the student quickly added, "She helped herself instead of having anybody else help her. That appeals to me more than having a man rescue her." Another young woman echoed this message of empowerment: "She wasn't the helpless female. She was more modern." Although this student had previously said that Viola was always speaking to her "as a woman," she was also impressed by Viola's convincing performance of a man. "I think Viola could pull off being a guy," she stated. Of Sebastian's abilities, she said, "I don't think he could pull off what she did. I don't think men can pull off what women can anyways." Despite the fact that she seemed to read Rourke's production as an assertion of female superiority, however, this same woman reported to me that her fiancé loved the production. Even though he had not read the play and never before attended theater, she said he felt he could "still totally understand what was going on."

The nearly universal appeal of this production for my students spanned an age range of more than twenty years, as well as different backgrounds, races, and countries of origin. My returning student, who said that she felt the production asked, "Who am I? What am I supposed to be? Who am I expected to be?" seemed to feel a profound connection to the show. Perhaps these questions of identity resonated with her because they reflected her own evolution. She was, at the time, in the process of remaking her life. After raising two children and getting divorced, she was returning to college in her forties with the goal of becoming a teacher. For her, even attending the theater felt like a reclaiming of her destiny, an assertion of her future. *Twelfth Night* was her second CST trip. During intermission, I found her in the lobby. "This is my new life!" she exclaimed.

For this student, a new life, engaged with theater, engaged with Shakespeare, leaves room for many different kinds of viewing. In arguing for Rourke's new millennial feminist gaze, I do not wish to discredit the infinite varieties of spectatorship available at any given time in the Windy City. However, I think my students identified in Rourke's production a specific appeal to a new generation, one appreciative of Elizabethan language, costume, music, and humor but also anxious to feel an intimate connection to the stage. They wanted to see versions of themselves onstage, to look in the eyes of actors standing onstage, and even to feel the splash of action from the stage. They wanted to believe that Shakespeare may have considered the experiences of real women, even if his Viola and Olivia had been played by boys. Most important, they wanted to look on female characters with a contemporary understanding of gender. They welcomed a connection with Olivia and Viola, whose sporty, flirty, bubbly, sexually aggressive, and even bi-curious natures seemed as fitting to our century as their own.

NOTES

1. William Shakespeare, *Twelfth Night*, ed. David Bevington and David Scott Kastan (New York: Bantam Dell, 2005), 2.3.2–28. This is the edition with which I teach. All further references appear parenthetically in the text.

2. Charles Spencer, review of *Much Ado About Nothing*, by William Shakespeare, directed by Josie Rourke, Crucible Theatre, Sheffield, *Telegraph*, September 30, 2005.

3. For more on the idea and production of the pool, see "*Twelfth Night*: Designer Lucy Osborne: Preparing for Water," Chicago Shakespeare Theater, accessed November 20, 2011. The website also includes a link to a time-lapse video of the construction.

4. *Oxford English Dictionary*, 2nd ed. (online version, September 2011) s.v. "feminism," accessed November 17, 2011.

5. Jenny Coleman, "An Introduction to Feminism in a Postfeminist Age," *Women's Studies Journal* 23.2 (2009): 10–11, accessed November 15, 2011, *Academic Search Complete*. Coleman also discusses the total rejection of the term *feminist* as associated with anti-male, anti-family agendas (11).

6. Ibid., 11.

7. Samuel Park, Review of *The Tempest*, and *Twelfth Night*, directed by Josie Rourke, *Shakespeare Bulletin* 27.4 (2009): 598, *Project Muse*, DOI:10.1353/shb.0.0117.

8. Ibid., 598.

9. Dennis Polkow, Review of *Twelfth Night*, directed by Josie Rourke, Chicago Shakespeare Theater, New City Stage, *New City*, April 6, 2009.

10. Chris Jones, "Unsinkable Shakespeare; 'Twelfth Night' Makes a Splash at Navy Pier," *Chicago Tribune*, April 6, 2009.

11. Jonathan Baude (Lead Guest Service Associate, Chicago Shakespeare Theater), discussion with the author, November 18, 2011.

12. "Facility and Virtual Tour," Chicago Shakespeare Theater, accessed November 17, 2011. For further discussion of the dynamics of the Chicago Shakespeare Theater space, see Jonathan Walker's essay in this volume.

13. This comment came from class discussion in the first weeks of April 2009, as do some of the other student comments referenced. However, I also interviewed seven former students and one student's friend regarding their memories of the production. Those interviewed included two male students in their mid-twenties; a male student around thirty at the time of the production; one woman in her forties; one woman in her late twenties at the time of the production; her friend, also in her late twenties at the time of the production; and two women of traditional college age, both now twenty-one. All interviews were conducted between June and November of 2011, two years after our trip. I have provided necessary information about each speaker in my prose, but I have refrained from citing individual interviews in order to provide anonymity.

14. Baude, discussion, 2011.

15. The Jentes Family Auditorium seats five hundred. "Facility and Virtual Tour."

16. According to Baude, CST further courts young patrons with $20 tickets for patrons under thirty-five.

17. "*Twelfth Night*: A Conversation with Designer Lucy Osborne," Chicago Shakespeare Theater, accessed September 30, 2011.

18. Jean E. Howard, "Crossdressing, the Theatre, and Gender Struggle in Early Modern England," *Shakespeare Quarterly* 39.4 (1988): 432.

19. Nancy Lindheim, "Rethinking Sex and Class in *Twelfth Night*," *University of Toronto Quarterly* 76.2 (2007): 682.

20. Lisa M. Anderson, "When Race Matters: Reading Race in *Richard III* and *Macbeth*," in *Colorblind Shakespeare: New Perspective on Race and Performance*, ed. Ayanna Thompson (New York: Routledge, 2006), 92.

21. Ibid.

22. Zac Thompson, Review of *Twelfth Night*, directed by Josie Rourke, Chicago Shakespeare Theater, *chicagoreader.com*.

23. Polkow, Review of *Twelfth Night*, *New City*.

24. "*Twelfth Night*: A Conversation with Designer Lucy Osborne."

25. While some of my observations regarding the performance are from memory, most are the result of viewing the DVD from the Chicago Shakespeare Theater Archive.

26. "*Twelfth Night*: A Conversation with Designer Lucy Osborne."

27. *Urbandictionary.com*, s.v. "emo boy," accessed December 29, 2011.

28. Howard, "Crossdressing," 431.

29. Ibid., 430–33.

30. Ibid., 431–33.

BIBLIOGRAPHY

Anderson, Lisa M. "When Race Matters: Reading Race in *Richard III* and *Macbeth*." *Colorblind Shakespeare: New Perspective on Race and Performance*. Ed. Ayanna Thompson. New York: Routledge, 2006. 89–102.

Coleman, Jenny. "An Introduction to Feminism in a Postfeminist Age." *Women's Studies Journal* 23.2 (2009): 10–11. Accessed November 15, 2011, *Academic Search Complete*.

Howard, Jean E. "Crossdressing, the Theatre, and Gender Struggle in Early Modern England." *Shakespeare Quarterly* 39.4 (1988): 418–40.

Jones, Chris. "Unsinkable Shakespeare; 'Twelfth Night' Makes a Splash at Navy Pier." *Chicago Tribune*, April 6, 2009.

Lindheim, Nancy. "Rethinking Sex and Class in *Twelfth Night*." *University of Toronto Quarterly* 76.2 (2007): 679–713.

Park, Samuel. Review of *The Tempest*, and *Twelfth Night*. Directed by Josie Rourke. *Shakespeare Bulletin* 27.4 (2009): 598. *Project Muse*. DOI:10.1353/shb.0.0117.

Polkow, Dennis. Review of *Twelfth Night*. Directed by Josie Rourke. Chicago Shakespeare Theater. New City Stage. *New City*, April 6, 2009.

Shakespeare, William. *Twelfth Night*. Ed. David Bevington and David Scott Kastan. New York: Bantam Dell, 2005.

Thompson, Zac. Review of *Twelfth Night*. Directed by Josie Rourke. Chicago Shakespeare Theater. chicagoreader.com.

"*Twelfth Night*: A Conversation with Designer Lucy Osborne." Chicago Shakespeare Theater. Accessed September 30, 2011.

"*Twelfth Night*: Designer Lucy Osborne: Preparing for Water." Chicago Shakespeare Theater. Accessed November 20, 2011.

6

Short Shakespeare! and the Corruption of the Young

JEFFREY GORE

Because I teach early modern literature, my kids experience it as a farmer's kids experience life on a farm. Since they've been young, they've known the Newberry Library as the place their father goes on Saturdays, and they knew the actress who would become Bellatrix Lestrange in the *Harry Potter* films as "the one who played Olivia in *Twelfth Night*." In the same way that running a farm can be an all-consuming activity for a farm family—where the adults care for children while they anxiously watch weather reports or fix the tire of a combine—the fact that my wife and I teach literature and conduct research at home as much as in the library creates for us a domestic environment where social studies textbooks, the Lemony Snicket series, and works by Borges and Renaissance playwrights seem to cover every horizontal surface by the end of any given week. I sometimes worry that I might be accused, as Socrates was, of "corrupting the young" for bringing up my children in a round-the-clock study hall. It is within this domestic milieu—and having usually just received our tax refund check—that my family becomes an obvious target market every spring for the "Short Shakespeare!" series.

As part of its educational efforts, each year Chicago Shakespeare Theater stages a seventy-five-minute version of one of the playwright's works. Set to begin at eleven o'clock in the morning, the "Short Shakespeare!"

performances give our family just enough time after the show to buy our children a Shakespeare pencil in the gift store before rushing them through the chain restaurants and souvenir kiosks on our way to a post-show lunch on the other side of Navy Pier. The performances regularly emphasize physical comedy and often truncate the longer speeches to a comprehensible length for an audience of attentive schoolchildren. But what impresses me most is the Q&A session that follows. It is clear that many of the younger members of the audience have gone through their own "corrupting" experience with an accompanying teacher who has organized the last month of classes around the hard work of digesting one of the plays and a Saturday field trip that just might change them forever. The fifteen minutes for Q&A after the show never seem like enough: there are questions about costumes, about how a favorite line was performed and what could have possibly motivated the "real Juliet" to have fallen in love with someone who wasn't even invited to the party. It's at this moment that I always feel we've actually gotten something right. This group of schoolchildren, who might normally be playing Nintendo or attending soccer practice on a Saturday morning, get to have an experience with their parents and schoolteachers, devoted actors, and everyone who is normally backstage holding together this messy "conspiracy" of education, entertainment, and a thriving cultural enterprise. And a few of them just might get hooked and become fans and customers for life.

In spring 2008, I was teaching *Romeo and Juliet*, and without a budget that semester for taking my students to the play, the stage at least seemed set for our family to see the Short Shakespeare performance of the play. My paternal strategies kicked into gear. I reasoned, the girls are too young to read the whole play on their own, but they'll likely enjoy watching the performance of it if they already know the story. So two family movie nights were devoted to films of the play: Franco Zeffirelli's version, to romance them with Renaissance dress, and Baz Luhrmann's *Romeo + Juliet*, to win "cool points" with our preteen, Lucía. As every teacher knows, however, it's a balancing act to show filmed versions of the plays: what if our students get caught up in various director's "tricks" but don't really listen to the lines or stop to think about what from the text might have motivated a particular performance decision? My daughters were fairly unimpressed with my assertion that Leonardo DiCaprio didn't really "carry the lines." And I had to admit that I was thoroughly captivated by Luhrmann's "fair Verona" set in a deconstructed Mexico City and by the sight of Claire Danes discovering the eyes of her Romeo through an aquarium. What if I had so stacked the deck that my children might feel let down when we actually went to see the play in the theater, with its relatively sparse scenery and no point-of-view shots?

As I would discover from the moment we entered the theater, this production had every bit as much of a "story behind the story" as did Luhrmann's Verona. The male actors in Amanda Dehnert's production were all marked with the Moko tattoos of the Maori people of New Zealand, and the illustrated playbills sought to educate us about both this Maori custom and about how different sets of markings served to distinguish the "two households, both alike in dignity." Every bit as captivating was the single item making up Tom Burch's set: an immense wrought-iron structure that could easily be adapted to form a city wall, a family tomb, a ballroom from which two "holy palmers" escape to share a first kiss, or a balcony for an ever-famous speech to be performed.

I'm always a little uncomfortable when the best-known lines from Shakespeare's plays are about to be spoken, even though I recognize this is genuinely unfair to the actors onstage. With the echoes of college freshmen anxiously repeating lines from soliloquies outside my office door (and of being that very freshman myself anxiously repeating the lines years before), each new performance runs the risk of being upstaged in my mind by the repetition of forced appreciation. Those lines such as "Friends, Romans, countrymen" from *Julius Caesar* have the advantage of being actual speeches within the plays. They don't sound so bad when they come off as deliberated, but by the time the words of a supposedly spontaneous soliloquy such as "to be, or not to be" roll off of Hamlet's lips, I often find it hard in most performances to believe that this truly "is the question."

When the wrought-iron ballroom twisted into a balcony, I braced myself as Romeo asked "what light through yonder window breaks?" The pressure to be genuine seems so much greater to the actor playing Juliet than it does for him playing Romeo, who has just been ridiculed by Mercutio for his forced rhymes—of "love" and "dove"—with the object of yesterday's desire, Rosaline. But when Lee Stark's Juliet looked out from the balcony to ask "Wherefore art thou Romeo?" on this March Saturday, the poetry merged with genuine spontaneity. She sounded thoroughly natural articulating the question, posed in simple syntax, about the very nature of what it means to be an individual and a part of a family. For the rest of the seventy-five-minute play, I completely forgot my role as father and educator. I was captivated by the scenery and the actors' command of the lines, and it was not until the lights came back on and the Q&A began that I stepped back into character. After the play we enjoyed mingling with the actors still in costume in the hallway, and I approached Lee Stark to ask her how she delivered such an oft-heard line without sounding overwrought. "Repetition," she told me. "I just repeat the lines over and over again and think about what they mean until they become my only way of saying it." She had totally gotten it right that day, and her strategy was not so far away from the pedagogical strategy of any old classroom I inhabited, either in the chairs or in front of the room.

As one of my daughters begins working on her first high school play, and the other fills her journals with the lives of countless characters, it is still impossible to know what will become of them as adults. I'm no more in command of their future than Juliet's father was of hers, and my daughters may very well become writers or actors or medical doctors or lawyers or dolphin trainers. And even so much as I proudly recall that my youngest daughter recognized over lunch at Navy Pier that Lee Stark's Juliet "spoke more beautifully" than did Clarie Danes's onscreen Juliet, it is admittedly I who was "schooled" on that March Saturday morning.

Doing Things with Words...
and, Sometimes, Swords

PETER SAGAL

Like a lot of middle-aged people with cushy jobs, I profess nostalgia for my starving artist days; but in my case, at least, I remember vividly hating it at the time. I wouldn't have minded the starving part if I hadn't been so hungry.

But of the many odd jobs I took to support myself until Hollywood or Broadway or somebody, somewhere, came knocking to save me from my obscurity, the one I enjoyed most was teaching Shakespeare to a group of retirees in midtown Los Angeles. My employer was a nonprofit senior center operating out of the former lunchroom at the top of the old May Department Store building on Wilshire Boulevard, a landmark of Modernist architecture that was almost abandoned when I walked inside in 1991. I had gotten the job from somebody I knew who gave it up for a better job; as I remember, his new gig was editing for a magazine for two hundred bucks a week. I could only dream of such riches and hoped that by jumping on his old rung of the ladder I could start my climb to glory as well.

My class was entirely female, as is common among seniors: men die sooner, of course, and those that remain were probably too busy watching sports or their stocks to bother learning about Shakespeare from a twenty-five-year-old aspiring playwright. I remember them as uniform in appearance and background—they were mostly Jewish women who had spent their lives in the surrounding neighborhood of Fairfax, and they all looked at me with the eager expectation of imminent learning.

I was afraid I'd disappoint them, of course. I had studied Shakespeare as a formal academic subject for only one semester in college, in a lecture course taught by the eminent English professor Marjorie Garber, and although just a few years had passed I couldn't remember a single idea she had intoned from the lectern. But I had acted Shakespeare a few times in college—I was a decent Bottom, so I was told, in *Midsummer Night's Dream*, and an overactive Antonio in *The Tempest*, but mostly and most importantly I was an aspiring playwright, and I wanted to teach and discuss Shakespeare's plays as plays: that is, as active, enacted depictions of human beings doing things. Shakespeare's genius, it seemed to me, was not so much his poetry as his sense of motivation, and how people acted upon one another.

So, facing the dozen or so deeply lined and eager faces, I talked about the great scenes of action in the great plays: not the battles, per se, but the scenes of characters acting on each other. I showed them act 1, scene 2 of *Richard III*, in which Gloucester encounters Anne escorting the corpse of her husband, whom Gloucester has killed, and ends the scene by seducing her into marriage. I broke down the scene, talked about Gloucester's stratagems, Anne's resistance, how he overcomes it. I talked about Gloucester's own amazement at his success—"Was ever woman in this humour woo'd? / Was ever woman in this humour won?"[1] and joked it might reflect Shakespeare's own joke about his own daring in attempting to write and sell that scene.

We did it again with five more plays, covering histories, tragedies, comedies, and romances. My appreciation of the playwright was not entirely without quibble. I might even have criticized Shakespeare for giving no final speech or action to Antonio in *The Tempest*, which drove me nuts when I acted the part. But we also talked about the great moments, the St. Crispin's Day Speech from *Henry V*, the brilliant act 3, scene 2 from *Othello*—"Honest, my lord?"[2]—in which Iago plants the seed of jealousy and destruction in Othello's mind by refusing to say anything, making Othello guess and guess more out of his darkest imaginings. And we discussed my favorite line in all of Shakespeare, meaning (because it's me) my favorite joke. It's from *Macbeth*, act 2, scene 2. Macbeth has killed King Duncan during the night and is loitering about the castle the next morning, waiting for the crime to be discovered:

LENNOX: The night has been unruly: where we lay,
Our chimneys were blown down; and, as they say,
Lamentings heard i' the air; strange screams of death,
And prophesying with accents terrible
Of dire combustion and confused events
New hatch'd to the woeful time: the obscure bird
Clamour'd the livelong night: some say, the earth
Was feverous and did shake.
MACBETH: 'Twas a rough night.[3]

Sure 'twas, Mac! I've seen dozens of productions of *Macbeth*, and not a single one of those has played that line for the mordant joke I believe it to be.

By the end of the six-week course, the ladies were excited and eager for each class, and so was I. Many of the women had been theatergoers their whole lives and told me of great productions they had seen twenty or thirty or even fifty years ago. Their enthusiasm for what I had to say, as personal and quirky as it was, made me even more enthusiastic to say it. They had never heard Shakespeare discussed in exactly this way, I think—as a writer for the stage, writing for actors, trying to move his story forward as convincingly and interestingly as he could.

This was years ago, and it makes me sad to think that all of those lovely, wonderful, curious women must now be gone. But Shakespeare endures, and these days I don't teach it anymore, but I watch it, and I take my kids to see it, including a few of the great "Short Shakespeare!" productions at Chicago Shakespeare Theater. I like them especially because when you cut Shakespeare skillfully you end up with the essence of the action, the people doing things to each other with words and, sometimes, swords (my kids like the word parts more, I'm happy to say).

Shakespeare, for all the reams of scholarly books and concordances written about his work, was meant to be acted. He was a playwright who made his living by putting doublets in seats, as it were, so his plays are all—more than anything—incredibly exciting, if done right and done well. (This, by the way, is what makes me angry about the Oxfordians and the Baconiams and all the snotty experts who are sure somebody "educated" must have written Shakespeare's plays. The Earl of Oxford might have been a true Renaissance man, but what the hell did he know about holding an audience's attention? You learn that by trying and doing and failing, in the theater.)

I don't take my family to Chicago Shakespeare Theater because it's good for them. I take them because Shakespeare, done well, is great theater, and great fun. Or so I was able to convince a roomful of nice Jewish ladies, two decades ago.

NOTES

1. William Shakespeare, *Richard III*, ed. Gary Taylor, in *The Oxford Shakespeare: The Complete Works*, 2nd ed., ed. Stanley Wells and Gary Taylor (Oxford: Oxford UP, 2005), 1.2.215–16.

2. William Shakespeare, *Othello*, ed. Stanley Wells, in *The Oxford Shakespeare: The Complete Works*, 2nd ed., ed. Stanley Wells and Gary Taylor (Oxford: Oxford UP, 2005), 3.1.106.

3. William Shakespeare, *Macbeth*, ed. Stanley Wells, in *The Oxford Shakespeare: The Complete Works*, 2nd ed., ed. Stanley Wells and Gary Taylor (Oxford: Oxford UP, 2005), 2.3.53–60.

16. Adrian Lester in Peter Brook's *The Tragedy of Hamlet* (2001), directed by Peter Brooke. Photo by Pascal Victor (Maxppp)

17. Cast of the National Theatre of Scotland's *Black Watch* (2011), by Gregory Burke, directed by John Tiffany. Photography by Manuel Harlan

18. La Comédie-Française's production of *The Imaginary Invalid (Le Malade Imaginaire)* (2004), directed by Claude Stratz. Photo by C. Doury

19. Chicago Shakespeare Theater and Carlo Colla e Figli's production of *Marionette Macbeth*, puppetry directed by Eugenio Monti Colla, actors and spoken word directed by Kate Buckley (2007). Photo by Michael Brosilow